Off the Map

Around the Dart, Avon and
Salcombe-Kingsbridge Estuaries

Jane Fitzgerald

with Trudy Turrell from
the Coast & Countryside Service

Photographs by Kate Mount

Published by Green Books with
the Coast & Countryside Service,
South Hams, South Devon

First published in April 2000
by Green Books Ltd
Foxhole, Dartington
Totnes, Devon TQ9 6EB

in association with South Hams District Council
and South Devon & Dartmoor LEADER II. This book is
part-funded by the European Regional Development Fund.

Printed by Kingfisher Print & Design Ltd, Totnes, Devon

British Library Cataloguing in Publication Data
available on request

ISBN 1 870098 83 8

Contents

Acknowledgements

This book really couldn't have happened without the support of Trudy Turrell and the team at South Hams Coast and Countryside Service. Trudy has not only contributed a huge amount of time and energy to the book, but has also shared her considerable knowledge of the locality, and slowed her pace during our many walks together. Ken Carter of the Coast and Countryside Service went through hoops to make this book happen—his support has been invaluable, as has that of Check McEwen of South Devon & Dartmoor LEADER II.

So many people have contributed to the making of this book that it is impossible to name all of them; however their help has greatly enriched it. I would particularly like to thank Kevin Mount, Rina Vergano, Ann Born, Ray Freeman, Ray Humphries, Pam and Graham Spittle, John Elford and Richard Allsopp.

Foreword

It all began with lamb stew. Some years ago we stayed in Dalgoed, a remote cottage in the Welsh Cambrian mountains. It was the middle of February. The house had no electricity—it was lit by oil lamps and heated by a woodburning range. Much of our energy was spent gathering wood for cooking, and making expeditions over the (small) mountains to the nearest shop to buy food, and heating the bath water in saucepans. A pot of lamb stew nourished us the week through. In the evenings, we read books in front of an open fire. Before we left, Richard wrote something for the visitors' book. Taking the form of a recipe, it recounted the journeys we had made, gathering the ingredients for the pot—the visit to the butcher, collecting wood, and the special greengrocer for the vegetables.

The recipe was left in Dalgoed's visitors' book, but the idea hung around. As it happens, *Off the Map* has turned out to be nothing like 'Lamb Stew in the Cambrian Mountains', but it owes something to it. For those who need them, *Off the Map* provides excuses and reasons to get out of the car—whether it be for gathering food from the hedgerows, canoeing down the Dart, or tucking into a hearty pub lunch after a strenuous clifftop walk. Equally, for hardier readers, who make expeditions as a matter of course, we hope that *Off the Map* will add substance, colour and local detail to your day.

Whatever your interests, *Off the Map* will help you along the way. However, it is not a prescriptive guide: rather, we hope that readers will create their own itineraries around the material in the book, and in so doing stumble across exciting discoveries of their own.

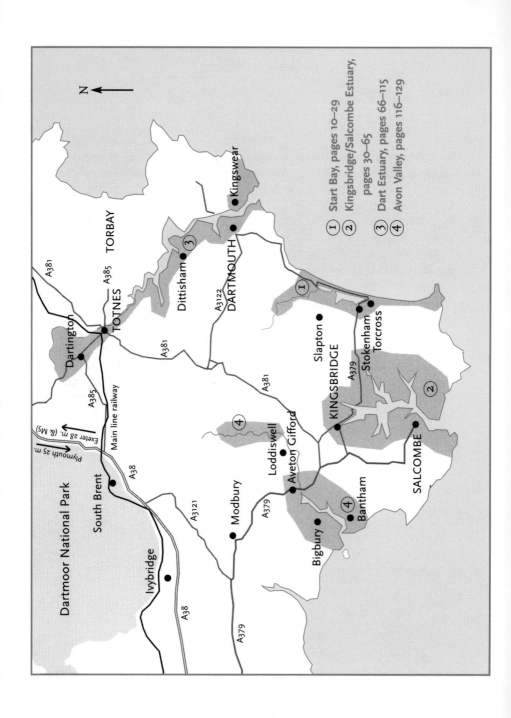

N

Dartmoor National Park

South Brent

Ivybridge

A38

A38

A379

A3121

Modbury

A379

Bigbury

Bantham

Aveton Gifford

Loddiswell

④

SALCOMBE

KINGSBRIDGE

A379

Stokenham

Torcross

②

Slapton

①

A3122

DARTMOUTH

Dittisham

③

Kingswear

TOTNES

A385

A381

A381

A381

Dartington

A385

Main line railway

Exeter 28 m. (& M5)

Plymouth 25 m.

TORBAY

A385

A381

④

① Start Bay, pages 10–29
② Kingsbridge/Salcombe Estuary,
   pages 30–65
③ Dart Estuary, pages 66–115
④ Avon Valley, pages 116–129

A Different Kind of Travel Book

Tucked between the slopes of southern Dartmoor and the sea, the South Hams is a land of river valleys. Five rivers define the landscape, threading through the hills and offering many a 'sheltered place'—which is the Anglo-Saxon meaning of 'ham'.

Before the advent of the modern road system, transport was much easier by water than through the high-banked twisting packhorse tracks. Each valley was quite remote and inaccessible, and so developed its own character. It is just these particularities of place that *Off the Map* tries to identify.

Although many of the remotest spots can now be reached by car, *Off the Map* encourages the reader to go at a slower pace. We suggest you visit one or two valleys in detail, and soak up the atmosphere through encounters with the people, by tasting local foods and enjoying the process of travelling itself, whether on foot, by bus, bicycle or boat. *Off the Map* is not all inclusive: it reflects one person's likes and interests. Superb places, businesses and activities have inevitably been omitted, and others will have changed hands by the time you read this book. I hope *Off the Map* will prove useful to dip into, and that it may initiate many eventful journeys of one sort or another.

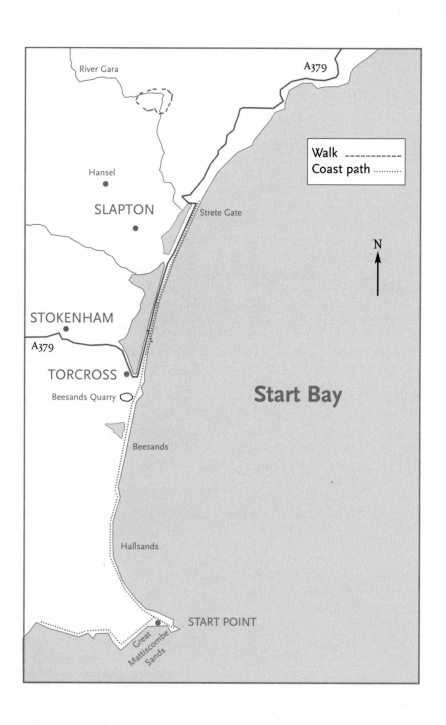

River Gara

A379

Hansel

SLAPTON

Strete Gate

Walk - - - - - - - -
Coast path ....

N

STOKENHAM

A379

TORCROSS

Beesands Quarry

Start Bay

Beesands

Hallsands

START POINT

Great
Mattiscombe
Sands

Chapter 1: Start Bay

This chapter covers the 4 km long 'line' or shingle
ridge between Strete Gate and Torcross. Detours are
taken inland to the villages of Slapton and Stokenham,
before continuing along the coastal path to
Beesands, Hallsands and Start Point.

The urge to race cars along the leyside road which runs the length of
Slapton Sands has something to do with the revelation of flat open
country, which forms such a contrast to a landscape veined with sunken
lanes, tall hedgerows and whaleback hills. This sudden encounter with
the very flat and the very long can trigger desires to run, fly, or otherwise
cover the distance as fast as possible—which is not recommended. *Off
the Map*, on the other hand, would suggest travelling by bus. For one of
the the joys of Start Bay is that it can be easily reached from both Kingsbridge and Salcombe, with buses running every hour.

Strete Gate

This is called after the gate which prevented cattle grazing along the shingle
ridge, and from straying up to the village of Strete. There was once an
estuary near Strete Gate, but now the River Gara is reduced to a small
stream which runs through silted marshland. The Manor House Hotel and
its tropical garden once stood on the sheltered site beside the car park,
which is now dotted with sturdy tables, cleared grassy areas and a barbecue.
Bring a butterfly guide, as all kinds can be spotted feeding on the buddleia.

On a raised mound is a viewing point which indicates landmarks to be seen across the bay: Slapton Line and Leys are clearly visible, as are the village of Torcross and the lighthouse at the end of Start Point.

Following the River Gara upstream from Strete Gate into the Gara Valley is impossible by foot, as the fields are very marshy. It is possible, however, to discover this remote and thickly wooded valley from the road which descends via the hamlet of Hansel.

The Gara Valley

The river Gara rises in high ground near Halwell, about six miles from its mouth. Its course runs though some of the most beautiful parts of the South Hams, through countryside mostly unchanged by this century. Around Hansel, a mile or two upstream from Strete Gate, the valley sides are so steep as to be almost impassable. Along its short course, which once powered five mills, are small stone bridges.

Gara Valley Walk

Land around the Gara is privately owned, but there is a wonderful walk to be had either by entering the valley on the Slapton side and following the lane down past Merrifield, or alternatively along past Fuge, off the Strete road. Walking in from the Slapton direction, follow the lane down for about one mile into the valley. After the sharp bend just past Hansel, a lane bears off to the right: this leads down to Lower North Mill and a small bridge which crosses the Gara. On the bank by the bridge, the ancient stone remains of some mill workers' cottages are visible. For those who lived here a century or more ago, everyday life here was both remote and hard, despite the beauty of the countryside.

After the bridge the path bears round to the left and leads back up the valley to 'Snail's Castle'—a house reputedly built for a Victorian mistress—perched on the cliffs overlooking the Gara. The cartoonist and impressionist painter Jack Yeats (see opposite) lived there at the turn of the century; his more famous brother, the poet and writer W.B.Yeats, and John Masefield, were both regular visitors. John Masefield's book *Jim Davis* (an adventure story for boys) is set in the valley.

The lane continues past Snail's Castle to Orestone—a house where the horses were changed after their long haul with flour from the mills below—and eventually leads to the Fuge road at the top of the valley. The gateway here opens on to a panoramic view of the valley, widening towards the coast. Alternatively, to end up on the Slapton side of the

WRITERS AND ARTISTS OF THE GARA VALLEY

Valerie Belsey, author of *The Green Lanes of England*, talks about some of the secrets held by the green lanes of the Gara Valley.

In the National Gallery of Dublin in May 1999, a gallery was opened, dedicated to Ireland's most famous painter, Jack B. Yeats. Amongst the sketches, water colours and oils, is an old sepia photograph taken at the turn of the century which shows Jack and his wife Cottie standing in front of their home 'Cashlauna Shelmiddy'—Snail's Castle in the Gara Valley.

Jack Yeats was born in Ireland, the son of a barrister turned portrait painter. At the turn of the century Jack married a Devon girl, moved down to Strete, and lived here for 13 years. Until then he had been making a name for himself working on black-and-white magazine illustrations for, amongst others, *Paddock Life* and *The Vegetarian*. His sketches showed great humour, something which was to be continued in his sketchbooks which deal with life in and around the Gara Valley. Yeats built a studio, now in ruins below the house, and spent his days sketching the valley, the sunken lanes, local fairs, circuses, races, shows and gypsies.

During his time in the valley he collected ballads and poems, which he published firstly through the Cuala Press, one of the most famous being John Masefield's 'Cargoes'. Masefield visited 'Snail's Castle' and wrote part of his novel *Jim Davis* there. Together they spent a lot of time constructing and racing toy boats along the Gara, both of them always dressed meticulously in suits and straw hats.

Although Yeats seemed to have lived a fairly reclusive life in the valley, there was one group of Strete residents who came into full contact with the great man—the children who attended the Strete National School (the building is now 'The Laughing Monk' restaurant). Jack and his wife were passionate about the theatre productions which were shown at the National School for the children at Christmas time. They had such thrilling titles as: 'Timothy Coombewest', 'The Wonderful Travellers' and 'The Gamesome Princes and the Pursuing Policemen'. The writers and artists of the Gara Valley had a lot to celebrate.

valley, take the lane down below Orestone that leads to Higher North Mill. Wild flowers are in abundance: orchids, highly perfumed white violets, and daffodils in spring. The turning back down to Lower North Mill is five minutes walk back towards Hansel from Higher North Mill.

A word of warning: some of the walking is rocky and steep; the rest is along quiet lanes. As there is nowhere to leave cars in the valley, parking in Strete would be recommended.

Slapton Sands

They may not enhance the beach outfit, but boots that come up to the ankle (or beyond) are best for walking the shingle beach at Slapton Sands. 'Sands' is a bit of a misnomer, for I doubt whether the shingle will enjoy sand status for a good few thousand years. On the other hand, this shingle does shimmer—and is golden, thanks to eroded flint fragments which somehow shifted to Slapton from the sea bed twenty-five miles away—and it doesn't get in your sandwiches. Mixed with the flint are granite fragments brought down from Dartmoor by the river Dart; also schists, slates and quartzite. At the north end of the beach, the rising cliffs provide some shelter. Along here stood the small village of Strete Under-cliffe, destroyed by the great gale in 1708. In the cliff face, some joist holes and the remains of a wall are all that are left of the village.

Even on warm days, Strete Gate is rarely crowded. The steeply shelving beach provides good swimming, and the water is clear and blue. Occasionally, more than the average acreage of flesh may be left uncovered, for the far end of the beach is still used by discreet naturists, although there is a more official site in a small cove further along the coast towards Blackpool Sands. In the late afternoon, with the sun declining to the west, there is a peculiarly clear, warm Devon light. Locals come down to unwind here after school or work, and no wonder.

Pictures of the Lower Ley

Slapton Ley

Slapton Ley is a National Nature Reserve. The Ley is a freshwater lake—the largest in south-west England—and is separated from the sea only by the narrow shingle bar, or 'line' as it is known locally. Slapton Ley is really two leys, a higher and a lower. The Lower Ley, an open freshwater lake with a thick reed fringe, is a well known pike fishery; and the Higher Ley is a lake now silted up with marsh and vegetation. The surrounding marshes and reedbeds provide excellent feeding and breeding grounds for all sorts of wildlife. Over four hundred and ninety species of plants have been recorded, including the nationally rare strapwort. Slapton is also particularly well known for its diversity of birdlife: ornithologists come to catch sight of rare migrants and other birds which stop off on their long and arduous flights. A sighting of the Great White Egret was recorded in 1994.

The Line—'The Barre of sand betwixt sea and lande', as the sixteenth century topographer John Leyland described it. Early summer evenings are the time to see the wild flowers at Slapton, with the wealth of

NATURE'S FLOTSAM

Anywhere between Torcross and Start Point you can expect the unexpected. Along the tide line are washed up all kinds of curiosities—the natural ones, not man-made plastics and tar. Look on the strands of seaweed and see the grey crustings growing on their fronds. These are sea-mats and sea-firs, colonial animals rather than plants; fascinating under a magnifying glass. Empty sea shells are there—oval trough shells and whelk shells, usually orange-pink and looking like giant, spired snail shells. If you see a ball of papery bubbles, these will be the egg cases laid in the sea by the whelks. White, oval discs, up to about 9 inches (20 cms.) long, are the chalky skeletons of cuttlefish. The brown or black purses, with tendrils or spikes sticking out from the four corners, are the cases where baby dogfish or rays developed. The brown ones with tendrils were laid by dogfish, and the black ones with spikes were laid by a species of skate or ray. The commonest are the purses of thornback rays. All of them are popularly known as 'mermaids' purses'.

different habitats created by the freshwater leys, the marshy ground, the reeds and the shingle ridge, which hosts quite different plants on the shoreward and landward sides. The yellow horned-poppy, sea radish, sea carrot, sea mayweed, restharrow and sea campion are the seaward varieties; landward species include viper's-bugloss, with its intense blue flowers, gorse and eyebright.

Thatching Reed has been grown at the Ley for centuries. It was cut and stacked in the autumn, for use in thatch, incorporated in cob buildings and for screens and garden fences. Before the construction of the road in 1856, the existing track was made more passable with reeds from the freshwater side of the line and with crushed shells and shingle from the beach. Each year, five acres of reeds are still cut by hand sickle and put into stooks in the traditional way.

PLANTS ON THE LINE

The plants along the ley and shingle bank are very colourful, and there are some unexpected species. There is sea radish. This is the tall, bushy plant, nearly waist-high, which covers large areas between the road and the ley. In summer it produces masses of small, pale yellow flowers. In autumn, greenfinches come to feast on the seeds in the swollen pods—and in summer so can you, for when the pods are small and tender they taste just like garden radishes. Nationally it is a rare plant, but here along the south-west coast it is abundant. In June, there are patches of bright blue, on both sides of the shingle ridge road. Walk up to one of these patches and you will see a forest of viper's-bugloss flower spikes. They are about two feet tall, with masses of blue, bugle-shaped flowers up the stem, with delicate, purple stamens protruding. Chris Riley has noticed that it flourishes particularly where he has cleared scrub in the cycle of clearance. Its usual habitat is chalk downland. What is it doing here? The answer is in the soil—or rather the shells in the shingle. The calcium from the millions of wave-broken seashells provides the requirements needed by viper's bugloss and several other calciferous plants that thrive along 'Slapton Line'.

Huntin', shootin' and fishin'   In the eighteenth and nineteenth centuries, the Ley was used for shooting, and there was an annual coot shoot in February to which most of the village turned out. In the 1920s and 1930s Slapton was a popular resort with wildfowlers and pike fishermen. The Royal Sands Hotel stood on the seaward side of the shingle ridge. An ivy-clad building with stone mullioned windows, the Royal Sands luxuriously accommodated shooting and fishing parties. Men and boys from Slapton village acted as ghillies, accompanying the guests and showing them the whereabouts of pike. In return they were given a beer at lunchtime and half-a-crown for the day's work. Pike—'of patriarchal age and size'—were displayed in glass cases in The Royal Sands. When Slapton was evacuated in 1943, the hotel had already fallen into ruin. It was finally demolished when 'Pincher' Luscombe, a collie from Slapton, triggered six land mines as he scrambled under barbed wire.

The Field Studies Council at Slapton Ley Field Centre manages the two hundred hectare National Nature Reserve which includes both Leys, the Line, deciduous woods and fast-flowing feeder streams. Herbert Whitely (the founder of Paignton Zoo) owned a large estate, of which the Nature Reserve was just a part. On his death in 1960, the estate was broken up, and the unproductive land—the Reserve—was leased to the Field Studies Council on the proviso that it be used for the dual purposes of conservation and education. **Slapton Ley Field Centre** thus came into being: it is a thriving centre of excellence, and runs courses which cater for a multitude of interests, throughout the year. 'Badgers and Bats', 'Myriapods', a 'Fungi Weekend', 'Slapton Safari', 'Tai Chi—inspiration from nature', 'Botanical Illustration' and 'Autumn Fruits and Berries' are just some of the many course titles which caught my eye when skimming through their programme. Courses need to be booked well in advance, and are primarily residential.

Chris Riley, the Reserve Officer, sees autumn as a good time to visit, both for the quietness of the place and for the extraordinary collection of visiting birds. To see the starlings roosting at the Ley is an eerie experience, with echoes of Dante (his image of the souls of the damned in the Inferno)—loud, gigantic clouds of them in their tens of thousands. Autumn is also the time for fungi, of which over 2000 species have been recorded in and around the Ley.

For the Passing Visitor The centre is a very friendly place. A welcoming reception area provides information on walks, fishing, recent bird sightings and forthcoming events. The Field Centre runs regular wildlife and mini-

beast safaris, and guided walks in
the summer; just call in there for
a leaflet. Opportunities for
walking around the reserve are
plentiful. The route around the
Ley is especially recommended
for those with young children, as
it offers plenty of distractions
along the way, such as contained
Leyside beaches, boardwalks,

SEA KALE

Slapton was noted for its sea kale, long
known in the south-west as a table
vegetable, but not introduced into
gardens until the mid 1700s. A certain
Mr Southcote of Stoke Fleming was the
first to cultivate it for kitchen use in his
garden in 1775.

bridges, and wildlife to be appreciated at any level—from insects to swans
to rabbits, and all free of charge. For fishing enthusiasts, clinker-built
rowing boats may be hired on the lower Ley for perch, rudd, roach and the
occasional pike. **Fishing licences** may be obtained at the Field Centre.
Slapton Ley Field Centre ☎ 01548 580466.

Slapton Village

In *A Fortunate Place*, his excellent book on Slapton, Robin Stanes writes:

> *Even as late as 1830 a resident remarked how remote Slapton was, how
> unsophisticated its people, and maybe it is this isolation that has produced
> the individual character and 'culture' of the area, the local breeds of cattle
> and sheep, dialect words, place names, and so on.*

In 1830 'H.V.D.' in Loudun's *Magazine of Natural History* noted that:

> *Totnes is the nearest place through which a London coach passes, which is
> about thirteen miles hence. Slapton is therefore seldom visited by persons
> from the metropolis, or in short by any travellers. The manners of the
> inhabitants are in consequence very unsophisticated; they are kind and
> hospitable beyond what we meet with in more polished society.*

It is no wonder that a drawbridge once protected Slapton village from
wandering Bretons. For, from the point of view of an early settler, Slapton
was a very good bet. In a site sheltered from the wind, with fertile soil and,
abundant supplies of water, as well as stone, wood and reed, and with fish
also in constant supply, the conditions were enviable. It is said that most
South Hams villages were self-sufficient in all but salt and iron. For
Slapton, iron was all that was missing. A remote place, some nine miles
from the nearest markets, difficult to reach by road, Slapton grew through
the centuries to be a fiercely independent community. Robin Stanes

includes several descriptions of Slapton's people in his historical account:

> *The presence of gentry had been scarce up until the seventeenth century,*
> *and from then on it was negligible. In consequence the village ran their*
> *own affairs and sorted their own disputes. This bred an independence of*
> *spirit, which has coursed through the generations to the present.*

Not all, though, were as independent (or wilful) as Lady Judith Hawkins, the lady of the manor at Pool who, when she walked to church at Slapton in the mid 1600s, made it her business to walk the whole distance along a red carpet, laid before her by two black servants to stop her shoes from getting muddy. She was 'remembered longest and best by the people of Slapton'.

With its narrow streets, earthy colours and tightly packed houses, Slapton explodes with flowers in springtime. Its sheltered position, soft climate and fertile soil allows for some splendid gardens and very early flowering. The waxen blooms of the early magnolias in Vale House and the secret garden of the Chantry are welcome beacons of spring. As I write, there are two gardens in Slapton which open on occasion to the public: Tor Wood, and Meadow Court.

The Chantry This terracotta-coloured building above the church, from which is slung the high footbridge over the road, is a later addition to the original collegiate chantry founded by local aristocrat Sir Guy de Brian in 1373, with the provision that on May 31 (St Petronilla's day) a funeral mass be sung for his soul. The Chantry was the last of its kind to be built in England before their suppression in 1545. All that now remains of it is the ruined tower, which can be seen from the garden of **The Tower Inn**, where at dusk on a summer's evening it is the perfect place to ponder the ancient stones of the tower and watch the resident bats dart in and out of the crumbling walls. **The Tower Inn ☎ 01548 580216.**

Below the Chantry is Slapton Church, dedicated to St James. Built of local Charleton stone in the fourteenth and fifteenth centuries, it is unusual for its spire, one of only three in the whole of the South Hams. Some of the seventeenth-century village cottages are still thatched, though the reed from the Ley is no longer in use. House repairs in the village have revealed the reed to have been in common use in the construction of cob walls. Shell fragments from the shingle are still apparent in the older renders, and the local stone is much in evidence in walls, coping stones and paving.

There are around thirty holiday cottages in the village, and during the tourist season the number of incomers equals, if not exceeds, the locals.

But the village still thrives, with its own community composting scheme and an excellent local shop—a visit to which is a must. It keeps local cauliflowers from Loworthy Farm in season, and other vegetables from local growers. Honey from the village is also stocked. For local events, look for notices on the bus shelter or in the shop. The horticultural show in August is not to be missed.

Start Bay Centre Housed in the old school building just outside Slapton, the Start Bay Centre is an educational field centre used by schools from all over. At certain times of year, during the school holidays, it may be hired privately by large parties. ☎ **01548 580321**.

Camp Site The camping and caravanning club site is noted as a fine site with very good facilities. It also has the advantage that both the beach and the Ley are a stone's throw away. A great base for exploring the area. **Camping and Caravanning Club Slapton Site, Sands Road, Slapton** ☎ **01548 580538.**

Horse riding at Dittiscombe Alex Farleigh runs a thriving riding stables at Dittiscombe, just beyond the hamlet of Pittaford outside Slapton. There are both indoor and outdoor schools. Lessons or hacks may be arranged at all levels. Riding is an enormously popular activity in South Devon, with events nearly every weekend. **Dittiscombe Equestrian Centre** ☎ **01548 581049.**

Torcross

Bang on the sea, the village of Torcross gets hit by the worst of weathers. The sea front houses line up stoically, scoured by salt spray, barely protected by the stout sea wall which rears up from the beach. In contrast to its sheltered inland neighbour Slapton, Torcross stands exposed at the south end of the Leyside drag. Until the 1600s it was probably no more than a cluster of fishermen's cellars, as before that time the threat of pirate raids made it impossible to live beside the sea. A fishing community then established itself and stayed. In his account in 1920, James Fairweather describes the scene as the women of Torcross pulled in the nets:

> *. . . from ruddy bright lasses to old dames of seventy years and upwards, whose bleached hair escapes from the great flapping sun bonnets which cover their heads They all wear painted canvas skirts, and stand holding a*

Torcross, beyond the water

rope. . . . A few minutes and the boat is up with a veritable boil in the
water, occasioned by the frantic gambols of the fish. The men pull a semi
circle round the school and quickly land on the other side.

Although one or two boats still work from Torcross, the fishing community has all but disappeared. Today, lone anglers dot themselves along the
beach, huddled over their lines.

Fish of the 'and chips' variety are immensely popular at the **Start Bay
Inn** at Torcross. The family who run this pub have made it their business
to do justice to traditional English fish and chips. The fish is locally
caught and fantastically fresh, the chips chunky and crisp. The trim-
mings are unpretentious, and sauces come in sachets. If you've come for
a more sophisticated meal, watch out for the specials on the black-
board—the skate wings and black butter is simple and delicious; so, I'm
told, are the scallops. The family room fills up rapidly, and can be rather
raucous, so get there early, for they don't take bookings. **The Start Bay
Inn, Torcross ☎ 01548 580553.**

Stokenham

A short distance from Stokeley
Barton Farm Shop is Stokenham, a
pretty village with a thriving church,
school and two pubs. Stokenham
has a burgeoning garden society,
whose plant sales are enormously
popular. The flower festival in
August makes a terrific show, with
the traditional leeks, chrysanths,
gladdies and spuds. The church also
puts on a flower festival which involves intricate assemblies of fruit,
flowers, seeds and vegetables. Another high point in Stokenham is the
local **Craft Fair** at the end of July.

Just about every aspect of the architecture of a village church tells a story.
Most are open to visitors (if not, ask in the local shop or pub whether it can
be opened up for a visit). The **Church of St Michael and All Angels** in
Stokenham is no exception. Records of 1198 refer to a church in Stokenham
dedicated to St Humbert. This changed to St Barnabas in 1786, and latterly
to the Church of St Michael and All Angels. Some details to note:

The Belfry The lofty west tower and peal of six bells has local blue slate
louvres in the belfry, in which the apertures are unusually wide to allow the

View from Stokeley Barton Farm

peals to sound out over what still is a very scattered parish. **South Porch** Cut into the stone work of the left hand door jamb is a rough cross, possibly a votive cross made by someone in the middle ages to remind them of a vow taken. **Holy Well** This was used to feed the church pond (where the car park now is). It is situated on the left hand side, above Church House. Its water was noted as a cure for eye disease. **The Sanctuary** A chair to the left of the altar belonged to a Reverend Henry Sherwood (b. Truro 1781), who had the distinction of being the first missionary to Persia, and translated the Bible into Persian. **Green Men** Built into the south wall is an early four-teenth-century double *piscina*, discovered during repairs in 1846. The brackets of the arches are carved with heads issuing branches from their mouths. **South Transept** The window shows the wreck of the 'Spirit of the Ocean', which was stranded on the rocks off Start Point on March 23rd 1888. Twenty-eight sailors drowned; they are buried in a mass grave near the lych gate at the top of the churchyard.

The Tradesman's Arms, Stokenham Handy for the church is this small uncluttered pub, perfect for a quiet drink or a rather special meal. Fish is particularly good here: the sprats starter is well worth a try. **The Tradesman's Arms, Stokenham** ☎ 01548 580313.

Torcross to Beesands

To walk southwards from Torcross to Beesands, take the Chapel steps on the seaward side of the Torcross Apartment Hotel. The route is marked with the coastal path acorn sign. The first bit is quite a climb, but at the top there's a terrific view along the sweep of 'The Line' back to Strete Gate.

Beesands Quarry

Before reaching Beesand Cellars, there is an opening which leads into a disused slate quarry. Once inside this vast steep-sided enclosure, the sands of the sea disappear and quiet descends,

SPRING GREENS

If you take a walk to Beesands in the Spring, why not pick your own salad or greens to complement the freshest of fish? Try a mixture of young dande-lion, corn salad, winter-cress, sorrel and young hawthorn and beech leaves—or try sea beet, a good substi-tute for spinach.

Sea beet grows in giant glossy clumps beside almost every seashore, estuary and river. Pick the youngest fleshy leaves—they smell and taste like spinach so it's easy to identify. Cook as spinach—there's no need to add salt as the leaves have their own salty taste. Lovely in a croissant, split and warmed with a little feta cheese.

SUNDAY LUNCH SHOPPING
AROUND STOKENHAM—THE FUN WAY

First gather your vegetables at **Stokely Barton Farm** shop, about a half mile walk up the road from Torcross towards Stokenham. A visit here can take as long as you want, for ' pick your own' is an option. My children love the activity of picking a crop and take great pride in their pickings. Strawberries in June are the favourite. It's a bit of a trek to the strawberry field, but worth every step for the view alone, as it stands high above the bay. Local Slapton pota-toes, Maris Piper in particular, are delicious roasted, and for those with large car boots, a sack or two make great presents to take back home. Also grown are King Edwards and Desirée. A detour to the plant area, where the collection of perennials and shrubs gets better and better, is recom-mended. **Stokely Barton Farm Shop, Stokenham.** ☎ 01548 581010. Opening times: Winter 9.30–5.30. Summer 9.30–6.30.

Set apart from the other shops at Torcross is **Hannaford's** the butchers. This family-run butcher's shop was part of the family farm. The shop has been in existence for 103 years and sells the best of local meat and game. There's no messing with pre-packaging here: the carcass is hauled down from its hook and the meat is cut in front of the customer. It's a friendly family business, known to give the occasional sweet to children on Saturdays (but that's a secret). Orders may be placed by phone. Hannaford's van calls at some villages. Ring for details. **Hannaford's, Torcross** ☎ 01548 580209.

Finally, cool off with a swim, throw stones at a stone tower, and bury as many feet as possible. For the more energetic, **sailing dinghies** can be hired from Torcross beach in the summer. **Contact Laurie Emberson, The Reeds, Torcross** ☎ 01548 580782.

Richard Hannaford, Torcross

interrupted only by the odd riff of birdsong or rustle in the undergrowth. A path leads along the quarry basin beside the remains of a pond which was once stocked with colossal goldfish. There follows a steep ascent (only suitable for confident climbers) to the rim where the coastal path is rejoined.

Beesands

This seaside village has undergone quite a transformation in recent years. The village green which runs behind the beach used to be dominated by a vast caravan park, packed with an army of green vans. Following their removal, Beesands has picked itself up and become a very desirable place to live. Nevertheless, it has utterly resisted being prettified, and held on to the look and feel of a working village.

The Bird Hide Past the houses at the north end of Beesands village, at the back of the green, is a small car park: there is a gate, and a short pathway which leads to Widdicombe Ley. Built on to the marsh is a bird hide, allowing intimate views of life on and around the marsh. The hide's existence is kept pretty quiet, and a visit to it feels like a privilege.

Shellfish Fishing was the mainstay of this small isolated community for centuries. Although this is no longer the case, the Hutchings family, who have been fishing from Beesands for generations, still run their fishing business from here. Fred Hutchings, a Beesander (known locally as Zanderlins) is the last remaining fisherman working all year round from

his beach boats. **Britannia Shellfish Ltd** supplies crabs, lobsters, crevettes and a host of other shellfish to some of the top kitchens in the country, including Gidleigh Park, The Horn of Plenty, The Carved Angel and the royal kitchens at Windsor. For the likes of you or me, wanting the odd crab or a kilo of mussels, Britannia Shellfish open up their tanks in the afternoon between 2.00 and 5.00. How much fresher can you get? For the lily-livered, the Hutchings will dress lobster or crab for you, but for this they

Angler fish at Beesands

need notice. Wet fish is also on sale when available. Opening times vary, ring to check. **Britannia Shellfish, The Viviers, Beesands. Office ☎ 01548 581186, Tanks ☎ 01548 581168.**

The Cricket Inn If ever a warm place was needed for refuge, it's on a cold day at Beesands. The Cricket Inn, on the front at Beesands, provides just this, with a welcoming roaring coal fire, and walls covered with photographs of old Beesands and its people. The fine ales on tap will revive the flagging visitor. **The Cricket Inn, Beesands ☎ 01548 580215.**

The Chapel The door to this tiny Edwardian chapel is usually open, but it has a very intimate and private feeling. On a wall inside is a memorial to villagers killed in 1942. Built almost on the beach, on a blustery day the strains of the elderly harmonium must be muffled by the breakers.

Hallsands

Stranger and stranger. Discarded machinery has been left to rust below the flight of steps which lead up to the **Hallsands Hotel**, which despite its rather unkempt appearance never seems short of business, for the clientele at Hallsands are concerned with elements other than the decor. Divers dock here at weekends, drawn by the logjam of the wrecks which lie on the sea bed. Hallsands Hotel also plays host to the auras of the annual Psychic Fair, as well as presenting hot jazz nights off-season,

when rooms are offered at a discount price. A practical place, catering for many people's needs—however out of the ordinary. **Hallsands Hotel ☎ 01548 511264.**

The ruined village of Hallsands, which was washed away in 1917, is visible from the coastal path, but it is no longer possible to walk amongst this mix of the domestic with the elemental as the path down to Hall-

Fred and Jean Hutchings bringing up the catch / The Cricket Inn

WIDDICOMBE LEY

The Devon Birdwatching and Preservation Society has built a hide behind the lake at Widdicombe Ley. A path goes from the car park, round the back of the ley to the hide. From it you have a grandstand view of mallard and coot, Canada geese and the resident swans. A pair of great crested grebes usually nest there. You are surrounded by the rasping, chattering song of reed warblers and may see one, a small, brown-backed bird perched on a swaying reed.

As well as mallard there are other duck. The diving duck are mostly tufted duck; the males are black and white, and their mates are brown. Slightly larger and less common are the pochard. The drake pochard are grey-backed with a reddish head and the females duck-brown again. Of the dabbling duck, the black-tailed gadwall and the chestnut-sided, shovel-billed shoveller are regular at Beesands. In midsummer, drakes of many species of duck lose their bright plumage and resemble their dowdy partners—this is called 'eclipse plumage'. By autumn the brown tips to the feathers are wearing off and the bright colours are beginning to reappear. In mid-September you may see the first wigeon, and some of the drakes will be just emerging from eclipse plumage and have beautiful pink and ginger tints. They are duck which nest mostly in eastern Europe and spend the winter with us. Not only do the drakes have striking colours, they also make an eerie sound—a shrill whistle which brings back memories of winter days on the estuaries and marshes of Devon.

sands beach has also been washed away. However, at the time of writing, a viewing platform is being built. 'The hamlet of Hallsands itself looks as if it properly belonged to the sea, and only been borrowed from it for a time.' James Fairweather, writing in his 1912 guide to the area, made an uncanny prediction of the village's fate.

Crowded on to this rock ledge were thirty-seven cottages plus a pub, shop and post office. The whole village was just forty feet wide. Almost all Hallsands' 128 residents were involved in fishing. Not only did the women haul the boats in, but also carried their menfolk to the boats on their backs so that they didn't start the day with wet feet.

Although the village had no harbour, a wide shingle ridge used to exist in front of this rocky ledge and this protected the houses from the sea. It was when the banks of shingle just offshore were dredged to make concrete for Plymouth's dockyards, that the shape of Hallsands beach began to change. The sea did not naturally replace the shingle, as the dredging company had promised, and after 650,000 tonnes of shingle were removed, the beach dropped by 20 feet, bringing the sea right up to the sea walls which protected the village.

SEADOGS

Newfoundland dogs were as essential to the fishermen in the villages around Start as the sheepdog is to the farmer. When the sea was too rough for boats to come close enough to throw a rope, it was the dog's part to fling itself into the waves and, thoroughly buffeted by the swell, swim close enough to the boat to grab hold of the rope between its teeth and swim back to shore.

After being battered by storms in 1903 and 1904, a combination of high tides and strong winds on 26th January 1917 brought the sea crashing into the village. All the cottages bar one were completely destroyed and the villagers left homeless. And now there is only one cottage and a few walls left standing, this remote fishing village is visited by students from all round the world; an object lesson in the effects of man tampering with environmental systems he doesn't fully understand.

Trout's Apartments are named after the sturdy Trout Sisters—Ella, Patience and Edith—who built the original Hotel on the proceeds secured through Ella, in 1917, having bravely rescued a sailor in difficulty. The sisters laid the foundations themselves, stone by stone. These leathery and legendary women caught their own fish and grew all the vegetables for their guests. After the deaths of Patience and Ella, Edith struggled to run the hotel on her own. It closed in 1959, but she remained there as a recluse for seventeen years—with the tables all set for dinner—until her death in 1978. **Trout's Apartments, South Hallsands ☎ 01548 511296.**

Start Point
Blackstone Rock lies off Start Point, as does the Skerries Bank—a shingle bank deposited by the shoreline currents. The two combine to make Start Point a notoriously hard stretch to navigate in bad weather: the sea bed is scattered with the wreckage of vessels which never made it. Walking

around Start Point needs care, for at places on the western side of the peninsula the steep rocky sides simply fall away into an often ferocious sea. The made-up road from the car park to the lighthouse is altogether tamer, and the going far easier. Whichever route you take, the blast of sea air, combined with the sheer power of the land and seascape, is very bracing.

Mattiscombe Beach At Start Point car park, beside the gate and stile leading in the direction of the lighthouse, is a path to the right. This leads down to Mattiscombe Beach. The walk down is about 15 minutes, and again it's important to watch children closely once through the gate at the seaward end of the path. Consult the tide table before a visit; low tide allows for more exploration, less fretful rock climbing, and space to play. It's a good beach for swimming, and some tame surfing. The walk down there filters out many less adventurous beachgoers, and I've never known it truly crowded.

KITTIWAKES

A new sound has been added to the waves and the wind at Hallsands. A few years ago the colony of kittiwakes moved from Start Point to the cliffs below Trouts, which echo with the birds' cries: 'Kitti-wake, kitti-wake, kitti-wake!' The colony has grown to several hundred pairs. Kittiwakes are proper seagulls, spending the winter out in the Atlantic, far from shore. In March and April they return to prospect for their nesting sites. In April you can watch the pairs building their nests on the vertical cliffs. They mould mud, muck and seaweed to cement a cup-shaped nest to the narrow ledges. The beaks are pale yellow, but the gape inside, when they open their beaks, is bright orange. Dozens of them sit on the ledges in pairs, nodding their heads and caressing each other's necks. When they fly off over the sea, you can see that the wing tips are completely black with no white specks. The legs also are black.

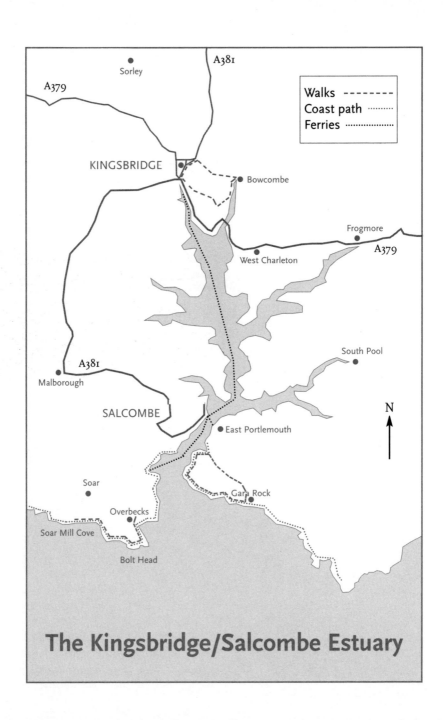

The Kingsbridge/Salcombe Estuary

Chapter 2: Kingsbridge/ Salcombe Estuary

This chapter takes a journey around the estuary from Salcombe to Kingsbridge, via the creeks of South Pool, Frogmore and Bowcombe.

Salcombe

History Salcombe has the air of an island: entering the town, with its jangling yachts and spiky vegetation, feels a little like going abroad. And it is just this separateness and comparative inaccessibility which makes Salcombe the distinctive place it is. By road, the journey is six miles from Kingsbridge, and to East Portlemouth on the opposite bank many more, via dizzyingly winding lanes. Traditionally, the way to transport goods and people back and forth to Salcombe has been by water, and with good reason—the route is infinitely more practical, enjoyable, and far shorter. Readers are urged to consider journeying at least one way by water, and the other by bus. At the time of writing, the bus ticket gives a discount on the ferry fare of 20 percent.

Exotic fruit Wine, fruit, cider, grain, wool, leather and timber—over the centuries these waters have seen all kinds of goods come in and out of the harbour. For Salcombe was a significant port, especially between the 1860s and 1890s, when oak from the woodlands on the banks of the estuary was transported by tugs to Evans, Bonker and Vivien, builders of the fast and elegant Salcombe fruit schooners. These skimmed across the

View of Salcombe

seas at terrific speed to the Azores and West Indies, manned by minimal crews who were seriously deprived of sleep (the less weight the boat carried, the faster it sailed and the fresher the fruit when it reached English shores). By the 1890s Salcombe was falling over itself with new houses and villas built by wealthy sea captains, and almost everyone in the town was involved in some way with the industry. There were ship-

wrights, carpenters, shipsmiths, riggers and sailmakers, as well as all kinds of ancillary professions: builders, schoolteachers, even dressmakers who sewed fine dresses for the sea captains' wives, using bolts of silk and cottons brought home from overseas.

Decline set in when the competition from the northern shipyards became too fierce. It was at this time that the emphasis switched from shipbuilding, fishing and shipping, to tourism.

Salcombe Haven The Marine Hotel was the first hotel in Salcombe. When opened in 1880, visitors were registered weekly in the local paper. The steamboat from Kingsbridge to Salcombe was the first pleasure boat to bring visitors to the haven—before then, Salcombe was only accessible to those with their own transport. At the beginning of this century the steep northern side of the South Sands valley, which had belonged to the Earl of Devonshire, was sold off in plots. Gradually, more 'pleasure boxes' were built 'in a cautious fashion'. Salcombe in 1929 was described in a guidebook as 'a pleasant retreat with a little harbour alive with scudding sails of tiny craft, and popular with delicate patients who appreciate bathing and beautiful surroundings'.

Lotus eating After the second world war, Salcombe attracted ex-officers with gratuities to spend. Some took up shell-fishing, while others bought luxury yachts for charter, cafés, pubs and restaurants.

The fishing that remains today is shell fishing: nine boats still operate from the fishing quay. The catch is mainly crab, spider crabs in particular. These are shipped off to France, where they are eaten as a delicacy. Otherwise it's mainly recreational fishing: out to sea for mackerel, or along the estuary for flounder, ray, trout and bass.

Figurehead in Island Street

Onshore at Salcombe

Exploring the town Approaching Salcombe by road, there is a steep pitch down into town. Glimpses of what's in store can be caught between the trees: sparkling blue water, fingers of distant creeks—and so many boats. As the harbour gets closer, so do the houses, muscling in on precious views of the sea and estuary—it is an extraordinary setting. The natural harbour around which the town has developed lies at the entrance to the sheltered Salcombe/Kingsbridge Estuary, either side of which are stretches of wild coastline.

The illusion of being on board is strong in this seaside haven, for even the rock on which the town is built is sea-green. Houses here borrow liberally from boats, assuming girls' names, with weather-boarding, flagpoles, lookout points and lifebelts gushing petunias.

One way to get a sense of the place is to explore the 'back doubles': a network of steps and paths cut into the steep rock, by which it is possible to traverse the entire town. It's a great way to keep fit, and an opportunity to catch those visceral views of backyards, gardens and workshops. For a breather, why not visit the **Holy Trinity Church** on Church Hill, where the tapestry kneelers have been painstakingly sewn by parishioners. Flowers, local scenes, association emblems, and naturally a lot of fish, boats and water: a parish map for knees.

Try to make time to visit the **Salcombe Maritime Museum** at the Council Hall in Market Street, below the Tourist Information Centre. This small museum run by local volunteers is stuffed with ephemera and information on Salcombe maritime history. There is a lot to see, so give yourself plenty of time, but beware of the French-style lunch hours. Bring your magnifying glass, as there's so much detail to soak in, stories to read, knots to learn and models to wonder at. **Salcombe Maritime Museum Council Hall Market Street ☎ 01548 843080.** Open Easter until the end of September, 10.00–12.00 and 2.00–4.00.

THE SALCOMBE ALOE

In the garden of Cliff House in 1774, the first American Aloe (a stately exotic) on record bloomed. The flower stem which shot out from the 28 year old plant grew at a rate of 9 inches a day, until at the end of September it reached 28 ft, bearing innumerable flowers on 42 branches. Its leaves were 9 ft long and 6 inches wide.

The library, council offices and Salcombe Yacht Club are all based at **Cliff House**, a splendid Victorian building. The gardens below offer a lovely public space for reading the papers having a picnic or simply watching the boats on the estuary. **Cliff House, Cliff Road, Salcombe.**

Beside the Water

Beaches There's a ferry to South Sands from Whitestrand, and Millbay is accessible from the East Portlemouth Ferry (see Appendix). As its name might suggest, the sands at both North and South Sands are good for making castles. There is also safe swimming. Further seaward there is a cove with a small lagoon, good for spotting fish and edible crabs. Crabbing at Victoria Quay is a popular sport, and it's easy to get fixed up with a line and bait from the local fishing shops.

Sitting On a fine day, the Ferry Inn garden is ideal for watching the world float by. So too the Wardroom Café in Fore Street, and Cliff House Gardens.

Swimming in the Rain Maintain the illusion that it's warm and sunny beside the estuary, even if it's teeming down outside. **The Marine Hotel Waves Leisure Centre** is gloriously situated beside the water. There's a good sized pool, an exercise room, jacuzzi and sauna. Half-day tickets are very good value for a bit of luxury. And if you really want to go for it, why not book a massage too. On Sundays there's a 'Roast and Swim' offer. Swim off your roast before you eat it! **Marine Hotel, Cliff Road, Salcombe ☎ 01548 844444.**

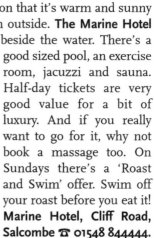

CRABBING

You will need: a crab line, purchased from any fishing shop; bait (bacon); a plastic bucket; and a high tide.

Sit on the edge of the harbour wall. Dangle bait into water pull them up and put them in the bucket. The person with the most crabs wins.

Tip them out and watch them all run back in the water amidst screams of delight from small children.

There's also a lovely 20-metre outdoor heated **swimming pool** close to the school in Onslow Road. Open from the beginning of May through to September, Mon–Friday 2.30–4.00 and 6.00–8.00 pm, Sat 2.30–4.00, Sun 2.00–4.00. Adults £1.50, children under 16 £1.25. Also available for private hire. **Contact Mr R. Sinnott ☎ 01548 843944.**

Crabbing at Victoria Quay

Salcombe

When shopping in Salcombe, be sure to bring a cool bag, for just below Shadycombe car park is the **Salcombe Dairy Ice Cream Factory Shop**, which stocks 'bin ends' of the local (and exceptionally good) ice cream. It might be a case of rum and raisin with only a smattering of raisins, or just an end of line; whatever the irregularity, it will be written on the box. Look out for cornets for children—masses of flavours to choose from—a small indulgence at 50p. **Salcombe Dairy, Shadycombe Road** ☎ 01548 843228.

Island Street, below Salcombe Dairy, is the centre for boat maintenance, building and equipment. There are chandlers with new and second-hand gear, tantalising noticeboards with an assortment of boats for sale, and craft for hire. Further along Island Street **Yeoward and Stone**, the place to pick up freshly caught crab and lobster. Thrill the children with a scary peek into the seawater tank in the warehouse!

A new addition to Island Street is the **Chocolate Factory**. This first started as a sideline for customers in Richard's Austro Patisserie in Fore Street (cake lovers

beware), but demand has increased so much that a factory opened last year. Try the handmade chocolates, which are made to a traditional recipe using boiled cream with blends of white and plain chocolates. **Yeoward and Stone, 14 Island Street** ☎ 01548 844261. **Cotons Continental Chocolates, Unit 1, Island Square, Island Street** ☎ 01548 844004.

Further along the street is the **Island Cruising Club Headquarters** (more about the Island Cruising Club in the *Offshore* section). Upstairs is the office, where courses, cruises and boats can be booked. Making your way towards Fore Street you pass **Victoria Quay**, a hot spot for crabbing at high tide. Lines and bait are on sale at the boat hire kiosk opposite. The fishermen's cottages on your right are amongst the oldest buildings in Salcombe. Now much prettied up, they'd set you back a yacht or two.

Under the bridge at the Fortescue, you'll see a set of steps leading up to the **Loft Studio**. Salcombe has a thriving community of amateur artists, and this is their base. It's always worth a look at the exhibition. The quality of the work is mixed, but sometimes there are paintings of such

exuberance, humour or sharp observation, that you're strongly tempted to buy one—at a very fair price, too.

Go over the road from the loft and turn left: a little way down is **The Oil Seller**, which stocks a profusion of things to make you feel good. It is also possible to book an indulgent half-hour or hour of aromatherapy treatment here. **The Oil Seller, 10 Clifton Place** ☎ 01548 843003.

Back on to Fore Street (the main shopping street in Salcombe): there's a lot of space given over to marine clothing. Sights are set on the 'yachties', and collections are certainly up-market, but you pay for the clothes to be hardwearing, practical and high performing. So if you want to invest in a Musto, Helly Hansen, or a pair of Soliado deck shoes, where better to do so?

For a present with a difference, why not choose one which has been across the world and back? Jon Alsop, a local sail-maker, had the bright idea of recycling used sails in the form of hardy bags and jackets. The range can be seen in **Ocean Spirit, also** in Fore Street. **Jon Alsop Sailmaker, The Loft, Croft Road** ☎ 01548 843702.

Up past Lloyds Bank is **The Tree House**, a toyshop that's a bit out of

Salcombe

the ordinary. It holds a diverting stock of toys, puzzles, games and tricks, assembled by a man who seems to have a direct line to what children want,

not what granny and grandpa think they want. **The Treehouse, 61b Fore Street** ☎ **01548 844133.**

Generally, food is expensive in Salcombe. There are no large supermarkets, except for a **Spar** shop at the top of town. At the bottom of town, **The Kitchen Garden** is a good friendly general food store. **The Upper Crust** bakery sells home-baked bread and wholesome pasties—a good place to stock up for a picnic. There is also a traditional butcher, and a fish shop where you may pay a little over the odds, but you can be sure of quality and freshness. **The Kitchen Garden, 80 Fore Street** ☎ **01548 842331. The Upper Crust, 3 Fore Street** ☎ **01548 842824.**

Eating Out

Eating out in Salcombe is patchy. I would avoid the smaller cafés, where quality and ambience are unremarkable, and all-day breakfasts can set you back the price of a small dinghy.

Opt instead for the places with the coveted views; there isn't a huge difference in price. The **Wardroom Café,** for example, overlooks the ferry departure point. Here one can linger over coffee and home-made cake, while watching the comings and goings on the water.

The Austro Patisserie, a small coffee house beyond Lloyds Bank on Fore Street, serves patisseries: mille feuilles and the Swiss Almond tartlet are favourites here.

Used by locals, and recommended for an inexpensive lunch, is the **Victoria Inn.**

At **The Island Cruising Club** in Island Street, lunches are served to non-members either in the bar or out on the waterside terrace. Sunday roast is good value, as are the varying dishes offered at lunchtime. **The Austro Patisserie, 61 Fore Street** ☎ **01548842511. The Wardroom, the Waterfront** ☎ **01548 842620. Island Cruising Club, Island Street** ☎ **01548 842329. Victoria Inn, Fore Street** ☎ **01548 842604.**

Hotel Food

Investigate the larger hotels, for they are much more accommodating to the casual visitor than might be expected. The South Sands, Tides Reach, Bolt Head and Marine Hotels all offer light lunches, with a range of pasta, soups, hot meals, filled baked potatoes and sandwiches. I compared sandwich prices, and they were on a par with (and in one case cheaper than) local pubs and cafés. Add to this the delight of sitting in style and comfort overlooking the estuary, and it's a strong option.

For atmosphere and a bit of jazz some nights, **Dusters** is a lively bistro, serving imaginative dishes including very good pasta. **Clare's Restaurant** is a bit more pricey, but the quality of the food is high and it does a super range of fish dishes.

Children always enjoy a trip to **Captain Flint's**, which does a great home-made pizza—fun food in theatrical surroundings. **Dusters Bistro, 50 Fore Street** ☎ **01548 842634. Clares Restaurant, 55a Fore Street** ☎ **01548 842646. Captain Flint's Restaurant, 82 Fore Street** ☎ **01548 842357.**

Terrace of the Wardroom Café

Out from Salcombe

Salcombe has three ferries in operation in the Summer months; here are some options for exploring the area using a mix of bus, ferry and leg power. The first is a coastal walk from Soar Mill Cove via Overbecks and South Sands to Salcombe itself; the second a visit to Yarde Farm near Malborough. Finally there's a ferry trip to East Portlemouth and a walk along shaded leafy tracks to the Gara Rock Hotel, returning by a spectacular stretch of coastal path.

1. Soar Mill Cove to Salcombe Town Centre
(via Bolt Head, Sharpitor and South Sands: a four-mile coast path walk.) Soar Mill Cove may be reached by the Coast Hopper Bus in the summer months—check times at the local Tourist Information Centre.

This walk covers a spectacular stretch of National Trust coastline. From Soar Mill Cove, follow the track to the coastal path towards Bolt Head. Owned by the National Trust, this section of the coastal path makes for comparatively easy walking, without the heart-stopping drops found on other parts of the route. Along the way, rugged rocky outcrops rise from short sheep-cropped grass. In late spring, spires of foxgloves line up amongst the gorse, and on warm days the air is thick with butterflies. Watch out for grey seals on the rocks below.

The stark promontory of Bolt Head offers splendid views towards Prawle Point, a good place to pause before descending into the valley behind Starehole Bay, where the shadow of the

WILDFLOWERS

Walking along the cliffs around Bolt Head you'll be stunned by the wealth of wild flowers. Identifying them is fun; I recommend bringing a guide. Taking them home is also possible, but not through yanking out roots and bulbs from the cliff-side hedgerows and meadows. Instead, drop in on South Milton Fruit Farm. Here Pam Gregson's wildflower seeds, bulbs, plugs, and pots of wildflowers are on sale. There are flowers and plants to suit all conditions: marsh, meadow, woodland and coastal. She also has native trees and hedging—such a refreshing change from the repetitive stock wheeled out in so many garden centres.

Pam Gregson also has a stall at Kingsbridge market on a Thursday. **South Milton Fruit Farm** ☎ 01548 560303.

GHOST STORY

After a particularly busy day at Overbecks, Alan Scott Davis, the then curator, was locking up and doing his rounds of the rooms, checking that all was in order. From the gallery above he heard noises. He was convinced that the house was empty, yet the noises grew louder. They weren't footsteps—more one footstep, then a dragging sound. Scott Davis then realised that in his later years Otto Overbeck had suffered a bad leg which was permanently bandaged, and the sound was that of him making his own nightly tour of the house.

wreck of the Herzogin Cecile, lost in 1936, darkens the water; nearby a waterfall dives into the natural pool beside Bellhouse Rock. Moving up out of the valley, the path joins Courteney Way. The previous owners, the Courteney family, cut this path in the 1860s for their many shooting parties to make use of. They broke the tops off the vast rock pinnacles on the cliff top for walling—the local hornblende rock is comparatively soft, easily eroded by the salt-laden winds. Colours of the stone are grey or green, the green being more pronounced when the stone is wet. You'll notice it used in some of the old cottage walls around town. This is a fine place for birdwatching: peregrines nest in the cliff face, and gannets drop out of the sky, fishing for sand eels. It is home too for the little owl.

Nearing Sharpitor, the path becomes shaded by sweet chestnut and sycamore, and leads to the entrance of the National Trust property Overbecks.

Overbecks

When Otto Overbeck invented his electrical rejuvenator he believed it could tone and cure 'all illness with the exception of malformation and germ diseases'. He claimed the machine had 'practically renewed my youth. My age is 64 years, but I feel more like a man of thirty and I am mentally more alert'. When his quest for immortality of the body didn't succeed, Otto settled for being remembered as the man to catch the largest recorded carp, and on his

death in 1937 he left his house and gardens to the National Trust on the condition that it should be named Overbecks after himself. Fifty years on,

Overbecks House

signposts still read Sharpitor, and that name remains in local currency. Sorry, Otto!

The House Occupying a spectacular site, the house now contains Otto Overbeck's intriguing collection with local additions. There is a maritime room with artifacts, stories and pictures piecing together some of Salcombe's rich maritime history. In the Overbeck room is the rejuvenator, and a collection of 19th century dolls with disturbingly adult dress and features. The shells on show in this room were probably the mementoes of sailors, as are the examples of scrimshaw—the decorated ostrich egg and sperm whale tooth. Hidden under the stairs there is a secret room especially for children. It is full of dolls and toys, including the Overbeck family's exquisitely detailed dolls' house settings. A 15-minute ride on the rocking horse was a reward for the best pupil of the week in Salcombe School.

A further proviso in Otto Overbeck's bequest was that there should be a youth hostel as part of the estate, and so there is. Occupying a position that four-star hotels would die for, part of the main house is given over to the YHA. What better place to wake up in the morning!

The Gardens Christopher Lloyd, the garden writer, refers to Overbecks' gardens as having a 'too good to be true setting'. Terraced into the hillside,

The garden at Overbecks

AND THEY RUBBED IT WITH CAMPHORATED OIL . . .

Pick up a dropped leaf from a camphor tree in the gardens of Overbecks. Crush it and smell it. Wood from the camphor tree has a particular smell, a little similar to eucalyptus. The wood was used in China for making clothes chests—the perfume from the wood kept the clothes smelling fresh. It was said by a Salcombe vicar that soldiers serving in China ended up with one of two things: a camphor chest, or a baby!

60 metres above the estuary, and sheltered by woodlands and cliffs, the gardens enjoy a remarkably mild microclimate. Tony Murdoch, an exceptional and adventurous gardener, developed these eight acres over 25 years until his retirement in Spring 1999. Tender plants thrive and grow to spectacular sizes: the 70-year-old banana palms, the orange and lemon trees, the camphor and magnolias, including the vast *Magnolia Campbellii* planted in 1901, whose deep pink flowers burn into the hillside for a brief spell in early spring. In May, visitors might catch the sight of palm trees carpeted with bluebells, with a few scarlet spikes of red hot pokers glowing through. The season Tony Murdoch looks forward to is early autumn, when the tender perennial borders are a riot of hot colours with the boldest of combinations.

From Overbecks, continue down Courteney Drive, past the wood-clad chalet-style Bolt Head Hotel, to South Sands. To get back to the town, it is possible to walk along the shoreside road or take the South Sands Ferry to the ferry steps.

2. Yarde Farm

Yarde Farm is off the A381 road between Malborough and Salcombe. The 606 'Tally Ho!' bus stops at the Yarde Gate Nursery, just next door.

Yarde Farm is neither a museum nor a tourist attraction—rather a family farm which has had a lucky escape from last century's bouts of 'farm improvements'. On Sundays from Easter to September, Marilyn and John Ayre open their doors to those who wish to explore the Georgian farmhouse (with a selection of farm buildings dating back over a thousand years), its fields and orchard, and to have farmhouse teas. You won't find plastic packs of jam, or catering portions of milk on Marilyn's table—just varied flowered china, set out under the trees or around a long farm table, and home-made cakes and scones (if you're lucky, 'heavy' cake straight from the oven).

Visiting here is like taking a look in someone's attic. Family stories are all around, from the ceiling rose in the dining room—a symbol of secrecy in the civil war—to the 500-year-old oak door behind which Hannah Balkwill, with the aid of a blunderbuss, kept her sons from being taken to sea by the press-gang men.

Very few farms and manors have the amazing range of outbuildings which Yarde has—from the back of the house you can see a bakehouse, brewhouse and dairy, where the family's eleven servants produced almost everything they needed. These seem quite modern when compared with the Norman pillared barn beyond. Family ponies still use the barn; why change a thing if it's still useful?

Most delightful of all is Yarde's old orchard. Beneath gnarled trees, tiny shetland ponies graze. John Ayre can name many old apple varieties unique to the farm: Chadders, Greasy Butcher with its yellow oily skin, Ironside (so hard it keeps for over a year), and Doll's Eyes, a small pink child-sized apple. Beside these trees new progeny have been planted, grafted by the Coast and Countryside Service and proudly tended by the Ayres, who make their own cider.

Beyond the orchard a wet field stands, full of wildflowers and visited by rare cirl buntings, unchanged by pesticides, sprays and the ubiquitous DDT of the 1950s and 60s. These treasures are again a fortunate accident, for the field gateway is too narrow for a tractor to ever have passed through—it's left a tiny time capsule of how Devon's countryside must have been centuries ago. For details of opening dates and times contact **Yarde Farm ☎ 01548 842367.**

3. East Portlemouth to Gara Rock

(Five miles, with some uneven rocky ground.) This walk takes a route across the estuary and along a tree-lined carriage track to Gara Rock. The return trip follows the coastal path around the estuary mouth back to East Portlemouth.

From the ferry steps at Salcombe, take the ferry to East Portlemouth. Turn right along the lane at the top of the steps or, if the tide is low, walk along the beach. Follow the footpath past the National Trust car park and on to the track planted with lime trees for the Duchess of Cleveland, who owned much of the parish. There is a steady climb up to Rickham, where the track ends at a lane. Take the footpath opposite through the old green tunnel of trees into an open field. Cross the stile, and turn right to the **Gara Rock Hotel.**

THE CLEARANCES OF EAST PORTLEMOUTH

Now one of the most exclusive villages in which to own a house, East Portlemouth was in the last century a somewhat run down hamlet populated by sailors, fishermen and wreckers. Owned by the absent Duke of Cleveland, his agents informed him that as the villagers would not work the land properly and only cared for the sea, it was a needless expense to keep them as tenants. In something akin to the 18th and 19th century Highland Clearances, almost half the population was evicted and their cottages demolished, then the land was made into three large farms. In 1880 Portlemouth's plight came to the attention of the national press, and as a result the Duchess of Cleveland paid for the restoration of the parish church.

The Gara Rock Hotel makes a natural stopping point for refreshment, and is especially welcoming when the weather is foul, for scones and tea in silver pots are served in the oak-panelled sitting room, irrespective of whatever elemental mayhem may be happening outside. Positioned originally as a coastguard lookout, the hotel watches over a broad stretch of sea. It was Richard Jordan who purchased Rickham Coastguard Station and Lookout at a Kingsbridge auction in 1908, and he transformed it into a hotel over two generations. By the 1930s it was a stylish retreat. Today, the decor remains wonderfully preserved, and the hotel offers a taste of unexpected luxury on this fabulous and rugged stretch of coast. Once refreshed, if there's the time and the energy, drop down to the beach at Rickham. With rocks to climb and pools to explore, it's splendid in all weathers. **Gara Rock Hotel ☎ 01548 842342.**

To return to East Portlemouth, take the path which curves in front of the lookout. This leads to the coastal path, which in turn leads back to East Portlemouth. As with most of this stretch of coast, there are some hairy moments and this way is not to be recommended for small or wild children, or nervous parents for that matter, but it is a surprisingly level walk—without switchback cliffs—for such a spectacular stretch of coastline. This walk is given in greater detail in the Coast and Countryside series booklet *Walks around the Kingsbridge and Salcombe Estuary*.

St Winwalloe's Church, East Portlemouth, with its spectacular setting, deserves a visit before catching the ferry back to Salcombe. In the middle ages East Portlemouth was a significant port, with a flourishing shipbuilding industry. The village provided four ships and ninety men for the Crecy and Calais campaigns of 1346. It was wealth built up from this, as

HUMAN BAIT

An effective bait for trying to get those crabs and shrimps out from under the rocks is the human hand. Put your hand in the water, be very still and patient and wait. Soon, the curious inhabitants will venture out to investigate and feed off those delicious dead skin cells on your hand.

well as from fishing and farming, which funded the building of this fine fifteenth-century church, which is approached through a graveyard scattered with the graves of shipwrecked mariners and smugglers. One eighteenth-century tombstone describes the murder of Richard Jarvis of Rickham by his apprentice girl, who was later burnt as a witch.

Sarah Fox, in her writings on the South Hams, recounts an occasion in the 1700s when a furious storm was raging in East Portlemouth. At the same time a funeral service was in full swing in the church. This was interrupted by word of a shipwreck in the raging sea below. The church was deserted in a flash, save for the lone coffin. Mourners and vicar had hurtled down the cliffs to plunder what they could from the stricken vessel.

Offshore—the Estuary

The Offshore section suggests ways of enjoying the Estuary and exploring the creeks between Salcombe and Kingsbridge.

The Kingsbridge-Salcombe Estuary stretches five miles, from Kingsbridge through Salcombe to the coast at Bolt Head. It is not a true estuary, but rather a series of flooded river plains, its narrow winding creeks extending to the most unspoilt and secluded countryside. The estuary and foreshore is a Site of Special Scientific Interest (SSSI), the water being clear, sheltered and salty. It provides a rare environment for underwater plants and animals. Bird and marine life is diverse and prolific. Because of the exceptionally sheltered and saline conditions, some species have been found here at their most northerly recorded point. Beneath the mud are rare and extraordinary sea slugs and snails; one particular slug is so rare it remains unnamed.

Taking to the Water

Rivermaid The Rivermaid passenger boat runs between Salcombe and Kingsbridge (tides permitting). Estuary cruises are available at certain times around high tide. These go between Salcombe and Kingsbridge, around the creeks or, weather permitting, around the coast either side of Salcombe harbour.

Boat Hire Another option is to be independent and hire a boat from one of the several companies in Salcombe which offer this. Exploring the creeks at leisure allows more time for really discovering the places for yourself. Check the tide times before you do so, because much of the estuary is inaccessible at low tide, when 450 hectares of mud are exposed. You'll need a chart of the estuary, a tide table, and be sure to pick up an information leaflet from the Harbour Office at Whitestrand, which clearly delivers the do's and don'ts of the estuary.

Houseboats Another way of getting to know the ria (a glacial water-filled valley) is by staying on it: houseboats are available for hire, moored

Sailing at Salcombe

in the peace and shelter of 'the bag'—some ten minutes from the harbour by launch. The houseboats offer a different perspective to a holiday in Salcombe. Tides and light structure your days, and learning how to leap between boats and tie knots is an adventure in itself—not to mention the heron-watching at dawn, and being left utterly undisturbed. Definitely worth considering. Contact **The Salcombe Boat Company** ☎ **01548 843420.**

Sailing

From the entrance over the Salcombe Bar, all the way up to Kingsbridge, the Estuary offers sheltered water for sailing and boating, and is ideal for learning to sail. The Island Cruising Club—founded in 1951 by a group of sailing enthusiasts on a co-operative basis—has grown into one of the leading sailing holiday and sail training organisations. For the residential courses, participants stay on the floating base, Egremont, a converted Mersey ferry. Non-residents may also book courses, and there is even a creche to take care of the children. More extended cruises out of Salcombe in classic yachts are amongst the many other options available.

The ICC now hire Toppers, Picos and surf canoes from their base at South Sands. Experience is required.

Winter Sailing Invest in a good wetsuit and enrol on a winter course, for in winter the estuary is wonderfully empty, course fees considerably less, and there's so much space to learn in.

Cadet Courses Take advantage of living locally: enrol your children in the excellent cadet courses run for local members by both the ICC and the Salcombe Yacht Club. **Island Cruising Club** ☎ **01548 843481. Salcombe Yacht club** ☎ **01548 842593.**

Exploring the Creeks

Creek- and estuary-side villages are awkward to reach by road, because of having to follow an unwieldy route around the estuary, but a joy to visit by water (tides permitting).

Frogmore (or lake of frogs) heads a creek of the same name which is accessible by boat, one and a half hours either side of

TIDES

Be aware of tides—invest 50p in a tide table. Rivers and beaches are transformed by the different states of the tide. Low tide is the time to go rock-pooling—on a moonlit night you'll see the limpets moving about! Birds and fish populate the foreshore mud of the estuary at low tide.

GREENSHANK BAY

For me, Frogmore Creek means 'Greenshank Bay' and 'Diving Duck Reach', not to be found on the OS map. From Frogmore village follow the public footpath along the north side of the creek for about half a mile. Turn past the saltmarsh at Cleevehouse Bay, until the path and creek bend to the west. Across the creek is Greenshank Bay. As the rising tide covers the mud, greenshanks gather. They can appear almost white, their legs greenish-grey, their slender bills slightly upturned. At low tide, greenshanks work the shallows of the creeks, sometimes running through the water for tiny oppossum shrimps. They stay all year round on the Kingsbridge estuary, which boasts more resident greenshanks than any other English estuary.

Further downstream, a long reach curves round towards Halwell Wood on the southern shore. I call this deep water channel 'Diving Duck Reach'. It is rich in fish, crustaceans and other estuary invertebrates. Lowest tide reveals a forest of tube worms, orange sponges and grey sea squirts living in the mud at the water's edge. Goldeneye duck are common here, and red-breasted mergansers can often be seen diving in synchronised succession.

Ever since great crested grebes returned to nest at Slapton in 1973, some have come across to the estuary. They travel great distances underwater, and dive frequently, so it can be difficult to keep track of them. The little grebe, or dabchick, with powder puff stumpy tail, also winters here. As the tide begins to fall they dive among the floating seaweeds along the shore. In summer the only diving ducks are the flotillas of baby shelduck. The black and white adult shelduck are beautiful, but they can't dive. They nest in old rabbit burrows under the gorse bushes on Ham Point. In late May or early June the parents bring their brood—a straggling crocodile of about twelve fluffy black and grey ducklings down to the creek. In contrast to their parents, these pied cotton wool balls can dive at will, bobbing up with a shake of their tiny heads.

high water. This allows time to moor up and take a creekside walk. There is a Coast and Countryside booklet of walks around the estuary available in local shops, which includes a delightful walk following Frogmore Creek. Try to include a visit to **The Globe**, a friendly pub which is very welcoming to children. Down the road from the pub is Frogmore Bakery, which sells fresh homebaked bread, cakes, and gorgeous oozy chocolate croissants. **The Globe Inn** ☎ 01548 531351.

Frogmore Regatta The timing of the Frogmore regatta is dependent upon the times of high tide. Gloriously set on fields which flank the head of the creek, Frogmore Regatta is a laid-back event and tremendous fun. A donkey derby, rowing races, ram roast & cream teas combine to make a Saturday afternoon in early August disappear quite delightfully. Having browsed at the odd craft or produce stall, grab yourself a hay bale and something cooling to sip, and settle in to idle away an hour or two beside

SALTMARSH PLANTS

Downstream of the stepping stones at the head of South Pool Creek is a fringe of saltmarsh and even a saltmarsh island which grows a little more each year. In summer there is a fascinating progression of saltmarsh vegetation. There is something other worldly about saltmarsh plants. First to grow out of the bare mud are upright succulents, resembling miniature branched cacti—without the spines. This is glasswort (*Salicornia spp.*) so called for its early use in glass making—the plants were burnt and their ash added to sand in a furnace. Once glasswort has established itself around the outer edge of the saltmarsh, other plants follow: sea-plantain, sea arrow grass and saltmarsh grass all grow in South Pool, along with the delicate pink flowering sea-spurrey and sea-milkwort. In late Summer the mauve daisy flower heads of the sea aster with their yellow centres stand tall above the brimming water.

the water, watching others paddling furiously around the creek. Meanwhile there are children's races to exhaust the kids, and if competitions aren't their thing, there's plenty of field to charge about in. And you can enjoy the privilege of a trip up the creek for 50p.

South Pool

South Pool sits at the head of another idyllic creek. By water, this remote village is accessible for only an hour either side of high tide. Until comparatively recently, the village was virtually self-sufficient.

CROOKED CHIMNEYS

When you're next in Frogmore or West Charleton, watch out for crooked chimneys. Did you know that you can use them as a compass? For they face towards the prevailing south-westerly wind. But why? Because the lime mortar used in their construction has expanded on the damp side away from the drying action of the wind, thus pushing the chimney in a south-westerly direction.

Doreen Shepherd describes the traditional way of life in her book *South Pool: Portrait of a South Devon Village in the mid-twentieth century* (available in local shops). At that time, the village had its own school, church, chapel and shop—which was supplemented by a collection of visiting shops, including butcher Cleave (a farmer from Slapton, whose meat swung from hooks on his horse and cart); baker Seymour from Chillington, and Messrs Rudd and Prin from Dartmouth with their suitcases full of underwear. The visiting hairdresser was Mr Alf Moore from Beesands, but the permanent wave was (appropriately) the job of Mr Lenny Crimp of Kingsbridge.

Mains water and electricity were only introduced in 1949; before then, water was channelled from springs or surface streams into communal taps, which are still in place: at the top of the village opposite Mole Hill, and at Cliff's End. There is also one remaining water pump in Herring Street. You might well pass by a horse mount, a cart swing, a buddle hole for water drainage, a mangold hold and a milk stand. There is also mention of the light on the bridge, donated by a certain Mrs Halifax 'to enable her son, Gerald, who was given to heavy drinking sessions at the nearby Union Inn, to walk safely over the bridge to the house she had previously had built for him named Albert Cottage.'

Times changed. In 1968 the school closed, closely followed by the shop. In 1972 the post office closed and the Western National Bus service was withdrawn. Today, the gorgeous setting and collection of traditional thatch and stone cottages has made it prey to the tourist industry, with around sixty percent of houses being holiday homes. **The Millbrook Inn** is busy and boaty, and serves good meals. Either side of high tide are the busiest times. To avoid the crush, why not linger a while in the village; visit the fourteenth-century church with its 16th century screens painted with the story of St Nicholas, and carved with the head of a grotesque one-eyed imp above the pulpit. The network of green lanes and bridle paths around the village make for some glorious walks. **The Millbrook Inn ☎ 01548 531581.**

Kingsbridge

Kingsbridge serves as the market town for many outlying villages in the South Hams. Shops in and around Fore Street reflect the diverse needs of the rural community, and the local calendar is peppered with agricultural events.

KIngsbridge Town Judging from the fine views of the estuary seen from the top of the hill in Fore Street, it might be assumed that, like Salcombe, life in Kingsbridge focuses on the water. Not so, for surrounded as it is by soft rolling hills and fertile valleys, where small mixed farms continue to be the lifeblood of the community, Kingsbridge remains the vital centre for these small village farming communities as it has done since mediæval times. There are many and varied routes into the town from the numerous small villages which surround it: Buckland-Tout-Saints, Bowcombe, West Alvington, Churchstow, West Charleton and The Mounts, to name but a few.

The town is a typically Saxon shape, with houses facing the central spine of Fore Street, behind which lie narrow strips of land known as 'burgage plots'. Small passageways to the east and west of Fore Street meander through to the two main outer passageways: Eastern Backway and Western Backway, both of which follow the course of the old mill leats. The eastern leat from the River Dod has been culverted under-

ground, whilst the western leat still runs its course along the end of the gardens, where large blue slate stones form bridges across the water. Squeezebelly Lane is one of a number of charming passageways; as its name suggests, it challenges the wider form. In wandering around these back lanes which thread their way down to the leats to the east and west of Fore Street, notice the local slates, called 'shiners', which are put to all kinds of uses, including flagstones, wall copings, tombstones and paving stones. The decorative tiles hanging on the upper stories of some of the houses in the town is a further use of blue slate. It was hung as a cladding mainly as a protection against the weather, being quarried locally at Sunnydale, on the coast near Beesands, at Buckland-Tout-Saints, and Molescombe near Frogmore. The King of Prussia pub at the bottom of Fore Street has its slates arranged in a fish scale pattern around a curved outer wall which was shaped to allow carriages to negotiate the corner successfully.

The older gates, railings and bollards of Kingsbridge have a distinctive style characteristic of Lidstones, the local foundry. Lidstones also manufactured their own kitchen ranges. Most locals had a Lidstone; they were exported in great numbers to Newfoundland (through the 'cod' connection), where they can still be seen working today. They also manufactured tools and iron work for shipyards.

Farming and tourism are the main industries around Kingsbridge. In summer it isn't unusual for whole families to move into caravans so they can let out their homes to the holiday trade. On Saturdays, armies of cleaners pour out of the villages into the holiday houses for frantic change-overs. However, with the coming of September, a quiet descends upon the South Hams. Gone are the choked roads of July and August. It's a time when locals reclaim the beaches and enjoy the last of the

Tiling patterns in Fore Street / 'Shiners' bridging the leat in Western Backway / White Hart Passage

summer. It's also the time for fruits. Local apples start to appear on sale, field mushrooms give reason for early morning walks, and blackberries taste all the better for the scratches earned whilst picking them.

Starting with the Kingsbridge Show, and moving on to harvest celebrations, this is a busy time in the local calendar.

Kingsbridge Show   The Kingsbridge Agricultural and Horticultural Society hold the annual Kingsbridge Show on the first Saturday in September. The local community turns out in force for a day packed with events, demonstrations, and entertainment of one form or another. Modest prizes are awarded for a wealth of different classes of horses, ponies, donkeys, sheep and cattle. The edge of competition is in the air as the modest prizes are hard fought for. Trade stands are packed with local businesses offering discounts on this and that, and the craft tent is a great place to buy early for Christmas. The food tent draws the curious and the hungry

with tempting samples of local produce. For a moment's respite, visit the horticulture and homecraft tent and gasp at the wondrous leeks, heady dahlias, and fairytale cabbages. Then ponder upon 'the most humorous boiled egg, with or without accessories'. Rounding off the afternoon is the young farmers' tug-of-war, with brawny teams heaving ropes back and forth until one side finally collapses. **Kingsbridge Show, Borough Farm.**

Harvest Festival It's well worth noting the dates of harvest festivals in nearby churches (East Allington, West Alvington, South Milton, Churchstow, Loddiswell), for this is one time of the year when churches are certain to be buzzing. The celebration of Harvest Festival remains an important marker in the lives of local village communities, who put on magnificent spreads at harvest suppers held in village and church halls up and down the South Hams. The churches are bountiful, with arrangements of fruit, vegetables, corn, barley, hops and flowers—a far cry from my own suburban memories of the sixties, when harvest festival amounted to stacks of canned vegetables topped with an apple or two.

Kingsbridge Fatstock Show

Fatstock Another important date in the agricultural calendar is mid-December, when butchers shut up shop to come to the Kingsbridge Fatstock show. Beautiful beasts are brought to market to compete for much sought after prizes. Farmers turn out in their best tweeds, and there's a lot of talking and dealing to be done. Until recently, it was the time for the Christmas fowl to be shown and sold; this is still the case in Dartmouth, which holds its fatstock show in the market square.

Devon Honey David Wilson, the Secretary of the South Hams Beekeepers' Club, is the largest honey producer in the South Hams. From his home in Sherford he keeps 70 hives—producing, in a good year, up to two tons of honey. In honey circles, they say that out of ten years, two are good, two are bad, and six around average. The unpredictable Devon weather makes or breaks the beekeeper.

David Wilson has lived near Kingsbridge for nearly 65 years, and he remembers the time when most farmers kept bees (in straw skeps), not so much for their honey as for pollinating crops. They were invaluable in the apple and cherry orchards, and in the strawberry fields. Changes in the South Devon landscape have affected the honey bee: the disappearance of the elm, with its early flowering pollen-drenched catkins which were a valuable source of food, as were the hay meadows with spring grazing; and a hay cut in June allowed flowering plants to set seed, thus maintaining a high diversity of species. Thankfully the hedgerows remain intact, providing excellent and varied forage for bees. David's bees now pollinate fields of linseed, field beans and oil seed rape. The nectar from the oil seed rape produces a thin, rather bland-tasting honey, which is nevertheless useful in the production of creamed honey.

On the first Monday and Tuesday in August, the South Hams Beekeepers' Club holds its annual exhibition in Kingsbridge, market hall. It's a hive of information.

BUZZ WORDS

For instance, did you know:

• For every pound of honey, bees make eight million visits to a flower.

• Bees fly the equivalent of two and a half times round the world for a pound of honey. And all for around £2.00 a jar!

Local honey is available from: Nicholson's Wholefood and Health Shop, 12 Fore St Kingsbridge ☎ 01548 854347; Healthwise, 81 Fore St, Kingsbridge ☎ 01548 857707. David Wilson's honey is on sale at Hope Cove Post Office ☎ 01548 561249 and Frogmore Bakery & General Stores ☎ 01548 531236.

Kingsbridge

The joy of Kingsbridge is that it has maintained its small scale, and has thus largely resisted the arrival of high street chains. Shops are largely local businesses, and you can do virtually all your shopping in Fore Street. Kingsbridge is a no-nonsense centre, with functional, practical shops providing good service. Everyday needs are a priority.

Practical needs

Nicola's Do you remember those pleated polythene rain hats? Or those plastic macs which packed into a small poppered wallet? Nicola's might well stock them. They might stock anything, for stuffed into a small space are all manner of goods. This is the joy of Nicola's, from the joke plastic biscuit to swimsuits, jigsaws, ladies' skirts, and some very good sailing shoes and sandals. So, if there's something you've been on the lookout for, it's worth a try. **Nicola's, 74 Fore Street ☎ 01548 852248.**

John H Donovan and Son If you ask John Donovan 'the fourth' (the present owner of Donovan's China, Glass and Furnishing Warehouse) for an anti-macassar, he won't bat an eyelid. It's

their business to stock just about anything for the home—they even sell cup and curtain hooks individually! They've been in existence since 1873, and in their present premises since the end of the last century.

Donovan's caters for a stack of domestic needs. In the front of the shop is the china section, in the middle, linen, and in the back, kitchenware. Carpets and furniture are upstairs. I searched heaven and earth for fly strips, eventually finding them in Donovan's kitchen department, along with cotton mop heads—in all weights. A well-run family business; the next Donovan to take the reins will be Hazel 'the first'. **Donovan's, 49 Fore Street ☎ 01548 852342.**

Nonsuch Hanging on the rails of 'Nonsuch', a small clothes shop at the lower end of Fore Street, is the

'Muddy Puddles' range of children's waterproof clothing. Tough and durable, this very practical and colourful outdoor gear has been designed by someone who knows her mud—farmer's wife Susie Cullen of Ringmore. What began as a purely waterproof collection has grown to include warm socks, useful cotton boiler suits and fleeces at affordable prices. Ideal for outdoor-loving kids, Muddy Puddles clothes are available by mail order. **Nonsuch, 13 Fore Street ☎ 01548 852892. Muddy Puddles, Hingston Farm, Bigbury, Kingsbridge ☎ 01548 810477.**

One third of your body heat is lost through your head, so it makes sense to get a hat. Why not pop into **Milburns**, which is stuffed with sensible practical outdoor gear, and buy one of Claire McKillop's fleece hats. These colourful titfers are inexpensive and gloriously cosy. Children love the large paw-print designs. Claire McKillop also makes fleece scarves and neckwarmers from her workshop in town. **Milburns, 22 Fore Street ☎ 01548 853926**

A short walk from Fore Street in Wallingford Road is **Avon Farmers**. Don't be daunted by those fearfully

Kingsbridge

capable women seen tearing into Avon Farmers in huge muddy vehicles and loading up with sacks of feed, seed and weed (killer). Farming women don't hang about: their days, like their fields, are very productive. There are still plenty of working farmhouse kitchens round and about, churning out huge quantities of home-cooked food, dispatching cakes this way and that, and filling shelves with jams, chutneys and jellies. As well as being a great place to browse, Avon Farmers is a lifeline for many people who live around Kingsbridge. It specialises in pet and animal supplies, wellies and serious rain gear, riding garb, all kinds of tools, as well as some fabulous farm animal greeting cards made by employee Robin Thomas. There's no pussyfooting around with small quantities here: string comes by the mile and seed by the pound. Bunches of seedlings on sale give a helpful nudge to the inexperienced grower as to what goes in when. **Avon Farmers, Wallingford Road ☎ 01548 857321.** Directions: Turn right at the top of Fore Street into Duncombe Street. At the first crossroads, turn left into Wallingford Road (look out for the vegetable stall

in someone's front garden). Avon Farmers is about 100 yards along on the left.

Gifts

Pig Finca
'Items for happy living and an easy frame of mind'. Angus and Sally Ann, founders of Pig Finca, planned to live in Spain; they even had a place lined up there called Pig Finca. Plans changed, and instead they opened a shop in Fore Street of the same name. Bringing some of that Spanish sensuality to a rural market town has proved an unlikely but successful move. 'Things we like' are the only guidelines which define what is on sale. These include regular lines such as organic olive oil, olives and spaghetti, on the one hand, and an eclectic selection of music, from African and Latin to jazz and opera.

Then there are the 'blow ins' such as hand-made soap, simple shell earrings and clunky plastic fly curtains which come and go, giving locals the perfect excuse for repeated visits. Pig Finca closes from mid-January until mid-March. **Pig Finca, 105 Fore Street ☎ 01548 854221.**

Two markets
WI Market 'Where else can you buy green bean chutney?' asks Anita Donny, the South West representative for Women's Institutes Country Markets Ltd. For 'green bean chutney' is one of the South Hams' hottest sellers. 'Local produce for local people' is the catchphrase for the hugely successful WI markets held weekly in 500 locations throughout Britain: an annual turnover of £11 million is an awful lot of cakes. It's a sophisticated business, and quality control is firm. In Kingsbridge on Wednesday mornings, a small queue gathers beneath the town hall clock as it approaches 8.15. They are mainly regulars, awaiting the pick of the bunch, including cut flowers from the garden (lilies of the valley, bluebells and delightful arrangements of seasonal flowers). The selection of perennials is unusual, and

Craig and Jackie Franklin outside Pig Finca

Kingsbridge

fresh produce is quickly snapped up. The crafts, although a little heavy on the knitting side, have some exquisite pressed flower greetings cards, as well as hand-sewn ones.

Whatever is on sale at the WI market, you can be sure it's of the finest quality, complying with guidelines right down to the screw-top lid. Freshness is carefully monitored: sponges and savouries must be cooked the day before or on the day of sale, and fruit cakes by the beginning of the week. Unsold cakes and pies do not reappear. The selling of fish isn't encouraged, and neither game nor alcohol are licensed (unfortunately—roll on the day when damson and rhubarb wines can be on sale too). Incidentally, the WI market is one of the organisation's few activities in which men are included, as they may sell their produce. Certainly men are keen customers—and often

head the queue at the pie and cake stall. **WI Market, Town Hall, Wednesday 8.30 am–12.30 pm.**

Farmers' Market On the first Saturday of each month between 10 am and 2 pm in Kingsbridge town square (at the head of the estuary, adjoining the Quay Car Park) is the Farmers' Market. This provides an opportunity for local people to buy local produce from a local source, including local fresh food, drink and horticultural produce.

Things To Do in Kingsbridge

The Quayside Leisure Centre After years of strenuous fundraising, Kingsbridge finally built its own swimming pool, which opened in summer 1998. There is a 25-metre pool, and a shallow one for non-swimmers. The Quay Leisure Centre organises lots of children's activities at half terms and holidays, and there are squash courts for hire, a sports hall, a dance studio, and a well

equipped exercise room. **Quayside Leisure Centre** ☎ 01548 857100.

Visage Tucked up one of the delightful passage-ways which flank Donovan's China and Glass Shop on Fore Street, is Penny Milne's Visage Beauty Therapy Clinic. Offering all kinds of treatments, Penny uses only the finest of natural oils and lotions, and has the knack of making her customers feel (and smell) wonderful. Advance booking a wise move. **Visage, Myrtle House, Fore Street** ☎ 01548 856816.

Films
The South Hams Theatre and Arts Trust organises a weekly film showing in Kingsbridge Town Hall. This intimate cinema experience (including waits for the reel to be changed) might not be terrifically comfortable, but they show some jolly

good films: recent releases as well as occasional classic art movies and children's films. Plans are in hand to

Women's Institute market / A poppy seller / Vegetable stall in Wallingford Road

Kingsbridge

upgrade the cinema, which will be called The Reel Cinema, and will show films more frequently. Currently, showings are on Wednesday and Thursday evenings at 8 pm. Tickets cost £3.00 for adults and £1.00 for children. **South Hams Theatre and Arts Trust ☎ 01548 856636.**

Harbour House This fledgling arts centre near the quay provides welcome space for yoga and art classes, as well as holding small exhibitions. The airy upstairs space may be hired for functions. **Harbour House, The Promenade, The Quay, Kingsbridge.**

Coronation Park A short walk from the Quay car park, across the road which runs along the embankment, lies Coronation Park. This small, old-fashioned

recreation ground offers what a park should: swings and slides, a putting green, tennis courts, a small café with tables and chairs outside; and if you're lucky, cream-clad ladies and gentlemen clunking the afternoon away on the bowling green.

The Cookworthy Museum Housed in the old grammar school at the top of Fore Street is the Cookworthy Museum of Rural Life. Recent restoration of the seventeenth-century school building (with the later Victorian headmaster's house attached) has transformed the school into a sequence of airy exhibition spaces. The school hall, complete with imposing headmaster's desk and chair carved with the names of boys gone by, is home to an exhibition of the story of Kingsbridge. Local geology—the first exhibit—outlines the complexities of the many-decked geological sandwich which forms South Devon. This is clearly and simply portrayed through maps and clear text, and helpful samples of mica schist, green schist, meadfoot bed and Dartmoor slate. Many of the exhibits can be touched, and all are

quite without superfluous 'gismos'.

Also in the Museum is **Balkwill's Pharmacy**, with its countless pots, jars, tins and drawers of seeds, roots, leaves and powders. Browsing here may evoke familiar feelings for some.

Downstairs is the kitchen, with its local Burgoyne range. This room is filled with Victorian domestic gadgets and equipment. Outside are kibblers, cutters, crushers and bruisers—a complete collection of local farm implements from the 1920s and 30s, grouped together by season. The garden is also used for occasional 'special days' when local skills and crafts are demonstrated. Keep an eye out for these. Another important date is the Thursday before Easter—family day again, with lots of opportunity to learn about rural skills, and when the children make flower baskets with the help of the local flower club. **Cookworthy Museum, 108 Fore Street ☎ 01548 853235.**

Eating Out
Have you ever found yourself on holiday with children, trawling the streets in the early evening for something to eat, only to find yourself in that hungry gap when

Kingsbridge Town Hall

Kingsbridge

daytime cafés are closed, and evening eateries are only at the potato peeling stage? Kingsbridge is exceptionally well off for child-friendly eating places, where one can either eat in or take away, with good, reasonably priced food before 7.30 pm.

Giovanni's Italians have a way with children, and Giovanni's is no exception. A visit here is always an occasion: children are treated like adults, and waited on with aplomb. Details like personal pepper-grinding and parmesan sprinkling make it a little special, not to mention the 'real' chips, but please don't let child-free readers be put off. Open by 6.30pm, this family restaurant in Church Street turns out a magnificent spaghetti, as well as more elaborate Mediterranean fare. **Giovanni's, Church Street** ☎ 01548 856707.

Ken's Kitchen—Fish and Chips Open at 5 pm, Ken's Kitchen is known for the generous size of its portions. On sunny days, a takeaway can be enjoyed in the small public space (next to the bingo hall), above what was Dodbrooke cattle market. The raised walkway allowed farmers to view the cattle in the pens below. Children love to sit upon the carved wooden animals, bag of chips in hand. **Ken's Kitchen, Church Street.**

The Dodbrooke Inn A friendly pub, serving home-cooked meals—again, fish and chips a speciality, as are charcoal-grilled steaks. Sunday roasts are inexpensive and popular. Food is served from 7 pm, and families are welcome. **The Dodbrooke Inn, Church Street** ☎ 01548 852068.

The Balti House Not for the hard of hearing, this robust and popular establishment serves the 'after the pub' crowd, as well as parties. Early evening is time for the quiet meal for two. A definite plus is the 'bring your own' drink policy, with no corkage to pay. For those whose teeth are set on edge by the metal dishes, take-outs are available; free delivery within a five-mile radius for orders over £25.00. In Kingsbridge, free delivery for orders over £15.00. **Balti House, 7a Mill Street** ☎ 01548 857072.

Portlemouth Pastries Comfort food at its best: Portlemouth Pastries sells fine British pies, cakes and tray bakes. They offer the definitive treacle tart, a very Devon cider cake, and their pasties take some beating. If you're feeling adventurous, the almond and apricot pie takes the biscuit. **Portlemouth Pastries, 15 Church Street** ☎ 01548 854073.

Mange Tout When you've trekked all the way up to the top of Fore Street, pick up a deserved treat at this excellent little deli. Great for gathering ingredients for that special picnic from a fine range of meats, cheeses, patés and pies, complemented by moist cakes and wicked gateaux. The sandwiches are excellent—great combinations between the freshest of bread. These may be taken away or eaten in, for Mange Tout has a small café at the rear of the shop; but the high stools make it difficult to accommodate small children or those with disabilities. Outside, on the other hand, there is a small courtyard with tables and chairs (access to this is through the car park near the back entrance to King's Market). Plans are afoot for the occasional summer's evening opening—a welcome move. **Mange Tout, 84 Fore Street** ☎ 01548 852133.

Kingsbridge

Support your Local Crisp Burts Potato Chips—a small family business founded by Richard and Linda Burt two years ago—is based at the Parcel Shed in Station Yard. At the turn of the century, when the Parcel shed was used to send primroses, snowdrops, live rabbits and other fresh produce to London, the crisped chip was a rare luxury—indeed the fried potato had only recently become acceptable as part of the British diet. It was the invention of the mechanical potato peeler in the 1920s that made the crisp commercially possible. The mild year-round temperatures and the rich red soil make South Devon a traditional potato-growing region. Johnny Bowles from Slapton grows most of the Saturna potatoes used for Burts chips. These are hand-fried in sunflower oil (the name of the frier is stamped on the packet), then flavoured with sea salt, mature cheddar, hot chilli and lemon, or just left plain. These hand-made crisps can be found on the shelves of Mange Tout (see previous entry) at the top of Fore Street, or at Nicholson's Health Food Shop at the bottom. **Nicholson's Wholefood and Health Shop, 12 Fore Street ☎ 01548 854347.**

Sayers If you're tied to the house, caravan, or tent for that matter, and you fancy something rather special to eat, then Sayers might be just the ticket. Philippa Sayers will bring a meal to your home—the dishes really aren't the kind you'd rustle up for yourselves. A freelance Cordon Bleu-trained cook based at Elston near Kingsbridge, Philippa will turn her hand to any scale of occasion, from three hundred hampers to the most intimate of meals. Philippa's food looks, and is, simply gorgeous: her wedding breakfasts are truly theatrical. Scale this down to a small dinner party, and the attention to detail remains. With prices on a par with a good restaurant, and savings to be made on babysitters and wine, give it a whirl. **Sayers ☎ 01548 856714.**

Out from Kingsbridge

Using Kingsbridge as a base, there are many outings within easy reach: here are just three of them. Others can be found in the *Ramblers' Walks around Kingsbridge* leaflet, or the Coast and Countryside's *Salcombe–Kingsbridge Estuary Walks* booklet, which contains half a dozen new routes as well as an insight into the wildlife of the estuary.

1. Along the Estuary

A continuous walk along the estuary from Kingsbridge is hard to achieve without encountering stretches of main road. Instead, try taking a bus from the town square in Kingsbridge along the A379 towards Stokenham. The service is reasonably frequent. Frogmore and West Charleton make equally good starting points for walks, with the Charleton marshes providing opportunities for birdwatching, and Frogmore having well-marked public footpaths. There's a circular route outlined in the Kingsbridge estuary leaflet which takes in the foreshore, lime kilns, Geese Quarry and, for the final stretch, joins the green lane which was once the main route between Bowcombe and Frogmore.

If you're in Kingsbridge and you've done the shopping, the traffic's busy and you need a break, treat yourself to Walk No. 11 in the Ramblers Association's publication *Walks around Kingsbridge* [reproduced with kind permission of the South Hams Group of the Ramblers' Association]. This transports one quite dramatically from the centre of Kingsbridge to the utter quiet of Bowcombe creek. Three miles in all, the route is steep in places and sturdy footwear is advised.

2. Kingsbridge to Bowcombe circular walk (3 miles).

From Quay car park, cross the main road and take the narrow passageway by Harbour House, turning left into Ebrington Street. Go along behind the bingo hall and continue on the raised pavement towards Dodbrooke Church. Continue on up the hill, and turn right down the tarmac footpath by the phone box, past the church and between it and the vicarage. At

Bowcombe Creek

GEORGE MONTAGU

Two hundred years ago, at the top of the main street in Kingsbridge close by the boys' grammar school, there lived a very special naturalist— George Montagu. He had arrived in 1798 with his 'friend in Science' and mistress, Eliza Dorville. He was the first to describe the 'Ashy-coloured Falcon', now known as Montagu's harrier. He found it nesting on a hillside near Kingsbridge, and kept the young in one of his many aviaries until they were fully fledged. On the coast he identified the rock pipit, and was the first to describe the nesting habits of the wine-purple and slate-grey dartford warbler. But of all the birds he discovered, it is the cirl bunting that most links our time to his. He found it in 1800 at Tacket Wood, on the outskirts of Kingsbridge. Although they were known from the continent, no one had identified them in Britain before. Eliza engraved a drawing of the cirl bunting for Montagu's *Ornithological Dictionary*, which was published in 1802. Through the nineteenth and early twentieth century, cirl buntings expanded their range into Wales and northern England, but since then the range has contracted. Now there are less than 500 pairs, all in South Devon. Local farmers and the RSPB are working together to provide the grassy winter stubbles, less frequently trimmed hedges, and fields with an uncultivated fringe, which seem to favour the plant and insect species that the cirl buntings need to survive and feed their young.

Montagu shot many birds to examine them and preserve them. After his death, his collection was given to the British Museum; it even included birds he had shot during his service for Britain in the American War of Independence. He studied many other kinds of animals too: about seventy-five species of seashore creatures—shellfish, crustaceans, worms, sea-slugs and fish—were named by him, and he was the first to describe the bottle-nosed dolphin. Of all creatures he said, 'They also feel the impulse of love, the greatest dictat of nature.' In 1815 he trod on a rusty nail in his garden and contracted lockjaw. A few days after the battle of Waterloo, which had claimed three of his sons, he died.

the far end, turn left down the hill, and after a hundred yards or so turn sharply right down the valley to the farm. Continue past Washabrook Mill and then up a steep rocky lane. At the top you come to a T-junction with Buttville Hill.

Turn left, continue over the brow and descend along the track (sometimes muddy) to the road. Here you are at the head of Bowcombe Creek. Turn right along the road to Rose Cottage (note the lime kiln now used as a garage). Past the cottage, turn right up a rising footpath and continue climbing until you reach a stile. Soon after, you come into an open field. Keep straight on and walk along the lower part of the field with the hedge below on your left. Beyond the farm to the left there is a stone wall facing you; turn right up the field here to the slate stile in the top left hand corner. Cross the stile, follow the hedge and go straight forward, down the steps and into the lane. Cross over, and again go over the stile almost opposite, at the top of the steep field (Bag o' Maize Field). At the bottom of the field, cross the stile/gate into the road, and after a few paces turn left into the park, through which walk to the Embankment and on to the quay. These two routes are simple walks, but with quite a few ups and downs. The views are magnificent.

The South Hams Group of the Ramblers Association runs two or three walks a week; these average seven to nine miles. There are also shorter strolls at weekends. Non-members are welcome. A walks programme is available at Kingsbridge Tourist Information Centre. South Hams Group organiser: **Mr B. Fox ☎ 01548 561419.**

WHAT TO DO WITH SEASHORE FINDS

Quaysides and riversides can be particularly good places for finding glass pebbles and sea-worn china chips. Many interesting pieces can be found beyond slipways, and particularly around Bowcombe at low tide.

1. Put a collection of mermaid's tears (sea-smoothed glass pieces) in the bottom of a glass vase to hold flowers—or in a shallow glass dish on top of which you can put water, even floating candles.

2. String up anything with holes or a rough edge—which can be bound with a fine gauge copper wire—into a mobile. Two pieces of driftwood make good poles from which to balance your finds. String up holed limpet shells, small pieces of driftwood, even dried coloured seaweed.

Or try making earrings from small bunches of shells and mermaid's tears tied parcel-like with wire.

SWANS AT BOWCOMBE

At Bowcombe, walk down the lane beside the creek and you will probably see the swans. Thanks to Margaret and Peter Quick, those at Bowcombe Creek have had more success than most on the estuary. Although many swans nest by tidal estuaries, few seem to allow for the height of the tides. The high springs of mid-April, soon after the eggs have been laid, or mid-May, just before they are due to hatch, wash out many nests. The Quicks built up the nest at Bowcombe using an old pallet, and since then they have used a variety of materials to jack up the nest platform. As a result no swan has been washed out at Bowcombe for many years.

A few years ago, a pair began to construct a nest mound in the middle of the estuary, on a mud bank. As usual, the cob (the male) brought material, but it was the pen (the female) who shaped and built the nest. Several hours after she had begun, when the tide had risen and ebbed again to reveal the scarcely visible remains of the mound, the pen rebuilt it. For two weeks she continued rebuilding only to have her work destroyed by the next tide. That was an exceptionally foolish swan.

Recently, just ten days after the young had hatched, the Quicks were summoned to Collapit Creek. The Bowcombe pair had taken their family of nine the mile across the estuary, where they had found another pair with seven cygnets. The Bowcombe cob had attacked the Collapit cob, striking at him with beak and wings; he was bleeding from the head. By the time the Quicks arrived, the Collapit swans had retreated to the head of the creek, but in the confusion had been left with only three cygnets. The Bowcombe pair had sailed off with thirteen. Over the next weeks, five of the thirteen disappeared, but the remaining eight were raised successfully, as were the reduced Collapit brood. Most swans at Slapton, the River Avon and the Kingsbridge estuary have been ringed. If you see a dead swan with a coloured ring, please report the two letter code to the harbour office or Tourist Information Centre.

Bowcombe Creek Bowcombe, the northernmost finger of the estuary, is a place of bobbing boats and birdlife. Inland towards Bearscombe, the river cuts its way though picture postcard countryside, with classic farmsteads tucked between grassy meadows. Upstream from the bridge you will find a bird-viewing platform, also favoured by local artists; downstream from the bridge at the dinghy park there is a flat grassy stretch, ideal for watching the comings and goings on the water.

Bowcombe Cemetery A short walk along the main road towards Kingsbridge on the left hand side is Bowcombe Cemetery, and should it be on your mind to ponder over questions of life and death, this is the place. Obscured from both creek and roadside by a vast enclosure of trees, the cemetery is entered through weighty ironwork gates. Once inside this municipal  burial ground, it is hard to fathom what season it is, let alone the year, for it is entirely enclosed by vast evergreen oaks and Monterey pines. The rows of graves stand all the stiller between the flow of traffic on one side and water on the other. Pale blue ironwork benches that have seen better days are dotted amongst the graves.

3. Sorley Tunnel Adventure Farm

Turbo slides, go-karts, gladiator's course, climbing nets, dolphin dip and death drop are just some of the diversions dreamed up by Sara and Richard Balsdon at Sorley Tunnel Adventure Farm, between Loddiswell and Kingsbridge. As it's small in scale, keeping track of the kids here is a doddle compared to the larger adventure parks. A working organic farm, Sorley also concerns itself with farming issues: "Where does food come from?" "How has it been treated?" and "What are GM foods?" are amongst the questions answered in the Food and Farming exhibition in the Big Green Barn. Around the farm there are lots of animals for cuddling, stroking and feeding, and should you wish to ride, Sorley has its own riding school.

Upstairs, the **Loft Restaurant** serves good home-cooked food, using organic produce where possible, and at good prices. Try to leave room for their classic puddings. **Heron Valley** cider and apple juice, pressed just down the road, is on sale here, along with Blewitt's Beer, which is brewed in-house. On the other hand if you're cooking at home, why not order an organic vegetable box—Sara Balsdon at Sorley is the local agent for River-ford Farm vegetable boxes. Orders must be placed by 9.00 am Wednesday for Thursday collection.

Season tickets for Sorley pay for themselves after only three visits—worth buying even for short stays. Open April to December. Directions: Coming from Kingsbridge, turn left off the B3196 just beyond Sorley Cross. There is also a regular bus service. **Sorley Tunnel Adventure Farm, Kingsbridge ☎ 01548 854078 (Riding School & Restaurant ☎ 01548 856662).**

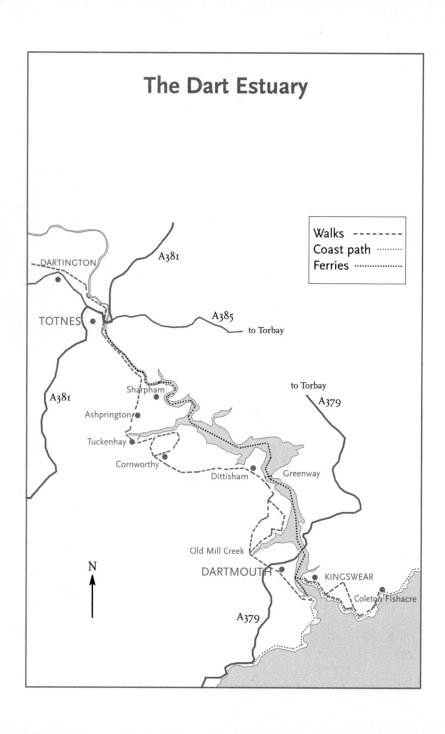

The Dart Estuary

Walks - - - - - -
Coast path ·········
Ferries ··················

A381

DARTINGTON

A385

TOTNES

to Torbay

A381

Sharpham

to Torbay

A379

Ashprington

Tuckenhay

Cornworthy

Dittisham

Greenway

Old Mill Creek

N

DARTMOUTH

KINGSWEAR

Coleton Fishacre

A379

Chapter 3—The Dart Estuary

This chapter tackles the Dart in the direction of the incoming tide, starting at Dartmouth and moving upstream through Dittisham, Cornworthy and Ashprington to Totnes and Dartington.

The ria that forms the **Dart Estuary** is the longest in South Devon. A journey down its length moves between contrasting landscapes: from steeply wooded valleys to rolling pasture lands; from broad stretches of deep water to the intimacy of hidden creeks, once the site of mills, which have cut their own steep-sided and secluded valleys. Although much of the woodland in the valley was only planted late last century, there remain some stretches of ancient semi-natural woodland, namely the National Trust's **Long Wood** and **Lord's Wood**. It was with oak from the banks of the Dart that the schooners for Dartmouth's Newfoundland fishing fleet were built. The name Dart itself means 'oak'. Such boatyards as remain are mainly for the repair, refitting and storage of boats, with a few exceptions: Pete Goss, for instance, is building his new racing yacht Challenger at Baltic Wharf in Totnes. The relative remoteness of the villages along the west bank of the estuary, the narrow lanes leading to them, along with the scarcity of flat land, has allowed them to escape any major development. Being relatively frost-free, the valley used to be known for its apple and plum orchards. Sadly, many have been lost, though much effort is being made to conserve and replant those which remain.

Dartmouth Castle

Dartmouth

The strong currents at the entrance to Dartmouth harbour diminish once inside the sheltered and almost completely landlocked waters at the mouth of the estuary. Daniel Defoe described Dartmouth as a port 'where five hundred sail can lie in safety'. The town's use as a haven and landing place is first recorded in Anglo-Saxon chronicles, and it was from these waters that boats departed for the Second and Third Crusades in the twelfth century. During the Middle Ages, Dartmouth established a flourishing trade with Brittany, Gascony and Spain, in wool, grain and wine.

From 1580 for around two hundred years it was the Newfoundland fisheries that bolstered Dartmouth's wealth. At its peak, hundreds of vessels left each March with a cargo of cloth, ironware and leather goods. Around a quarter of a million cod were caught in the waters off Newfoundland in a season. On shore these were gutted, dried and salted, and the oil pressed from the livers for use in the manufacture of soap and lamp oil. When the ship was full, it sailed to the Mediterranean, trading the salted

COAL LUMPERS

In the mid-19th century, gangs worked in competition with each other to refuel visiting ships. Runners were stationed at Compass point, who, when a steamer was spotted would run to tip off their gang who hung out on the embankment or Bears Cove. The first man to put his leg over the iron ladder on the wall of the cove won the right to moor the ship, and the first team to row to the ship won the contract to bunker it. These races were the forerunners of the Dartmouth Regatta's gig racing events.

fish with Catholic countries. Dried fruit and wines were brought back to England on the return journey. The houses along the Butterwalk, and other fine seventeenth-century buildings in the town, were built from the wealth brought to the town from the Newfoundland cod industry. A slump in trade in the late eighteenth century brought unemployment, poverty, over-crowding and disease. Things became only marginally better when, in the mid-nineteenth century, Dartmouth became a coaling station, fuelling visiting steamers in the Dart.

More jobs were created when the Navy established its floating training station in Dartmouth in 1863. Two wooden hulled warships, 'Britannia' and 'Hindustan', accommodated the cadets; there were also racquet courts, kennels for beagles, floating swimming baths and boat sheds at their disposal. However the overcrowded conditions on the warships prompted the building of the present Royal Naval College. Part of the Raleigh estate was compulsorily purchased, and the Edwardian College buildings, designed by Aston Webb (architect of the Victoria and Albert Museum), were completed by 1905.

Looking at the town from **Kingswear** on the opposite (eastern) bank, gives an idea how Dartmouth has developed, for all the flat ground where the shops are now was once submerged. Ray Freeman, in the publication *Devon Estuaries,* gives a picture of the changes undergone in this part of the town:

> *The Embankment which runs along the west bank of the river between the two car ferries is an example of how much of the town has been reclaimed from the mud of the river, the original bank of which was at least one*

hundred yards to the west. The Boat Float entered today under the bridge on the embankment, was before 1885 open to the river, and schooners could sail up to the quay. The Royal Avenue Gardens and Coronation Park to the north are both on what was once mudflats. Under the latter lies a submarine brought in and scrapped in the 1920s and buried when the park was landscaped in the 1930s.

From the eastern bank it is also possible to see how the town was originally two separate villages— Clifton and Hardness. These fishing communities were established in the eleventh century upon the ridges either side of an inlet which ran roughly along what is now Duke's Road. Surprisingly, the process of reclamation began as early as the thirteenth century, when this inlet was dammed, creating a causeway (now Foss Street) which led to a tidal mill.

Grapes and Gargoyles The streets of Dartmouth should be explored as they were intended: on foot or by packhorse. Eleven different flights of steps and alleyways course through this intricate and cluttered town: some of these are achingly pretty, others just plain dank. Horn's Hill and School Steps began life as conduits, taking the water from the springs in the hillside, cutting paths through the oldest parts of the town and allowing privileged views of some of the most interesting architecture. Much of it may be provincial and unsophisticated, but there are some terrific examples of local craftsmanship in all its vigour. Beasts, mermen and assorted monsters gawp from walls, pillars and doorways, around which scramble vines heaving with grapes. There's a riot of woodcarving, plasterwork, ironwork and mosaics out there. I have outlined below just some of what's on offer. A street map can be purchased from the Tourist Information Centre in Mayor's Avenue.

Woodcarving: St Saviour's Church in St Saviour's Square is one of the few buildings to survive from the

Dartmouth Embankment / Browns Hill Steps

fourteenth century, at which time the water lapped up to the east wall, to which ships were moored. It was over this wall that scolding wives were swung and ducked into the water at high tide. Built from wealth gathered by John Hawley from trading wine with Bordeaux, it was consecrated in 1372—although some of the fabric appears to be considerably earlier. Note the weighty door, primitively carved with lions, and the carved grapes over the altar. Guides available in the church give a detailed account of what can be seen.

The overhanging floors of **The Butterwalk** (1628–40) are also profusely carved, with quatrefoils, mermen, beasts and assorted foliage, as are the brackets. So too is the facade of 16 Clarence Hill, and in this instance the carvings are picked out in reds, blues and yellows.

Ironwork It was local foundries which produced ironwork for the town. A lovely example of its use lies in the finely proportioned **Morocco House**, one of a delightful sequence of houses along **Bayard's Cove**. The playful pink and white ironwork of the balcony reflects the appearance of most early ironwork: it was painted in bright colours until the death of Queen Victoria, when the Nation's ironwork was ordered into mourning and painted black.

Flock Tudor There was no shortage of work for local craftsmen when the grand houses of Fairfax Place were built in the 19th century. Their unrestrained façades imitate seventeenth century buildings as only the Victorians could, presenting riotous combinations of woodcarving and ironwork. Also note the floor mosaics—mainly black and white marble—in the occasional entrance way. These were laid by the Italian craftsmen who were shipped over with their families to make the mosaics in the Royal Naval College Chapel. These mosaics, so easily passed by unnoticed, were the results of their weekend work. A few Italian fami-

The Butterwalk

lies remained in Dartmouth, going on to open the ice cream parlours and fish and chip shops in town.

Icing on the Cake There are some splendid examples of Devon lime plasterwork in Dartmouth. Following the fashion of wall painting in the 1500s, when walls were presented in surprisingly bright colours, plasterwork ceilings and overmantles became fashionable; firms of craftsmen worked exclusively in this technique, using lime plaster mixed with fine goat hair. The influence was certainly Italian, but it was the Devon craftsmen, notably the Abbot Brothers from Newton Abbot, who developed styles unique to this locality. **The Butterwalk** has particularly fine examples of this work in its first storey rooms. These merchants' houses, built in the late 1630s, once backed onto the quayside, allowing owners to keep an eye on their ships from the back window. Look round the back—there's still an iron ring for tying the boats. The wood and stone carved fronts are lovely examples of work of that time. It's worth having a coffee in the **Sloping Deck Restaurant,** above the baker's shop, if only to see the fine plasterwork overmantle of the Pentecost scene.

Next door, in the room above **12 The Butterwalk**—now 'True Blue'—is a truly sumptuous plasterwork ceiling entirely covered by a Tree of Jesse. To view this, arrangements may be made to collect the key from the Guildhall ☎ **01803 832281.**

Water Thoughts
At a kiosk opposite the harbour office on the South Embankment is the office of **J. Distin Boat Hire.** The third generation to hire boats out of Dartmouth, Mr Distin has four traditional crafts to choose from. All are clinker-built with inboard motors, and are reassuringly stable for the novice. The smallest holds six comfortably, the largest, twelve. Perfect for taking your time to explore the Dart. **J. Distin ☎ 01803 835034.**

The River Link Realising the limited potential of a chug up the Dart with churned-out commentary, River Link is busy diversifying into themed trips, evening cruises with live music, gourmet beanos to Sharpham Vineyard, and more. Look on the embankment kiosks for news of such events. Boats depart from the Steamer Quay on the east

Mosaic in Fairfax Place

bank close to the River Link office. **River Link ☎ 01803 834488.**

Baltic Star This glass-topped boat works from Baltic Quay on the west bank, and offers an alternative way to view the river, with cream tea cruises and fish and chip suppers a favourite. **Baltic Star ☎ 01803 868811.**

The Water Taxi Run out of G & T on your yacht? There's nothing else for it but to call the water taxi. Richard Hawke can bring provisions to your boat without you ever having to step foot into Somerfields. Richard has an eighteen-foot Plymouth Pilot with cuddy; he can taxi up to ten people. Happy to transport would-be campers to appropriate and desolate sites up the river, and fetch them when the need arises, he's up for legal, off-beat commissions. **☎ 07970 346571.**

Meals on Keels Richard's brother David is a chef, who prepares cracked crab and lobster bonanzas for lavish picnicking on- or off-shore. His more down to earth (but no less tasty) dishes are available frozen for those who didn't get it together to order their shopping-by-taxi.

Cheemaun—the open canoe One of the newest vessels on the Dart is 'Cheemaun', the largest canoe in Europe. Twenty-six feet long, and painted bright red and yellow, this huge open canoe was built by Alan Bridges in Wales. Co-owner Phil Sheardown takes groups of up to twelve out on the river for the best part of the day for £80–100; he also runs two-person open canoes. Phil has the British Canoe Union's qualification, which allows him to take the public on open canoe trips up the Dart and to the Salcombe Estuary, as well as the waters around Plymouth and the Yealm. Picnics can be provided. Eco-friendly, and an exhilarating way to see the river. **Phil Sheardown ☎ 01803 865301.**

The Dartmouth Regatta

Still drawing the crowds annually at the end of August, Dartmouth Regatta first started in 1839 as a diversion for the very rich. Rowing was the focus of events, with sailing on the periphery. One hundred and sixty years on, and with a vast programme of events, the regatta draws all sorts: from the half million pound motorboat set to serious sailors, yachtsmen, rowers and scullers, to those who come just for the crack! From the moment the Mayor hands the silver oar to the Chairman of the

Dartmouth Ferry

Royal Dartmouth Regatta, until it is handed back at the closing cere-
mony, Dartmouth is one big picnic. Cars are banished from the streets,
allowing the town to be used in the way it was intended. Dartmouth
excels itself with this large scale extravaganza, making full use of the
resources provided by the many military retirees and others, all of whom
are used to running a tight ship.

Water Races Whaler, gig, skull, kontiki raft, dinghy, yacht—if it floats,
it races in regatta week. Local rowing events are hugely popular. The
regatta has seven whalers and seven blue boats which are brought out of
store for local teams to practise. Friday is local rowing day: competition is
ferocious, in particular the licensed victuallers' men's whaler race. Come
the evening, with races won and lost, the pubs are exceptionally lively.

Between the abseiling wall and the tennis courts is the **Craft Tent**, a
perfect opportunity to check out some of the best local produce and crafts
without rushing about the countryside.

Red Arrows For many it's a family ritual that ranks as high as harvest
festival or the County Show. There's a great feeling of holiday. Hours
before the display (usually held on the first Saturday of the regatta), families spill on to Dyer's Hill above the estuary. Picnics are produced, and
everyone settles in for a good evening. Burgers and hot dogs are laid on
for the less organised. At exactly six-thirty, a tiny glistening dot emerges
from the far reaches of the Dart. Seconds later, flying in exact formation,

the Red Arrows tear down the estuary,
blasting trails of coloured smoke behind
them. The Red Arrows have been
appearing at the Regatta since the late
seventies. It's a 'high' or 'low' show,
depending on cloud cover. The display
lasts around twenty-five minutes. The
cliffs, coastline, estuary and steep-sided
valleys provide a stunning setting for
the Arrows: the focus is drawn in as they
skim the water, and then out as they
burst skyward with stomach-pulling

verticals, which burst into cascades of colour over the fields and water
below. Afterwards, there's a couple of hours to spend at the fair before
dark, when the firework display begins.

Regatta Fireworks Getting a deck chair around the boat float on fireworks night is a bit like getting a ticket for the Wimbledon Final. It's not a

Dartmouth from Dyer's Hill

question of camping overnight, but certainly over tea. Families arrive around 4 pm, a good five hours before lighting the touch paper. Deck chairs cost £2.00 per evening. Firework displays are on Thursday and Saturday nights at around 9 pm—check out the programme.

ARROW TIPS

• Warning: the roads clog up hours before the show.
• Get there early.
• Bring binoculars and a picnic.
• Other spots for viewing include high ground in Kingswear and Dittisham.

Dartmouth Film Society

You need warm jumpers, blankets, and maybe even a sleeping bag for Dartmouth Film Society's alfresco screenings. Conceived back in 1997 over a cup of coffee, the Dartmouth Film Society is in full swing and winning prizes—namely the British Film Society's 'Best New Film Society' award.

'The real plus is that we don't have a cinema', says chairman Rob Bird. For taking film outside of the cinema was one of the hopes of the society at its conception. They have done just that, and screenings have included: 'Evita' at the Carved Angel, 'The French Lieutenant's Woman' at Bayard's Cove, and, most appropriately, 'Jaws' on the beach at Blackpool Sands! This proved such a hit that beach screenings have become a regular feature of the summer programme. The evening kicks off around 7.30 pm with a band, and the Blackpool Sands Café serves 'wondrous nosh'. After dark, under the stars, it's movie time. The Film Society also sponsors a number of one-off events on art and the landscape. Watch out for these. **Dartmouth Film Society ☎ 01803 835285.**

Dartmouth

As autumn sets in, Dartmouth boats are put into store, and the crowds start to thin. Out of season the pace is less frantic, and shopkeepers can give their customers more time and attention. Specialising as it does in the 'not immediately necessary' things of life, Dartmouth is a brilliant place for seeking out unusual gifts.

Books
The Harbour Bookshop (formerly owned by *the* Christopher Robin, son of A.A. Milne) will not only advise on books, but they will also order, gift wrap and mail a book of your (or their) choice complete with card. Beat that, amazon.co.uk!

For those who love secondhand books, the **Church of St Barnabus** on Newcomen Road is stuffed with yards of them from floor to ceiling. **Harbour Bookshop, 12 Fairfax Place** ☎ 01803 832448.

Clothes
And if you can't face shopping for clothes in big stores, Dartmouth is packed with small clothes shops, with lots of good names scattered amongst the rails of the small and friendly stores. **White Stuff** in Victoria Road has some wonderfully unrestrained shirts, fluffy fleeces, and

rangy sports gear. **Riverside Fashions**, on the other hand, make it their business to keep their customers warm dry and comfortable, and **True Blue** in the Butterwalk has clobber that's nautical but nice. **White Stuff, 11 Victoria Road** ☎ 01803 834070. **Riverside Fashions, Fairfax Place** ☎ 01803 832125. **True Blue, 12 Duke Street** ☎ 01803 835556.

Liquor
Dartmouth Vintners
With a history of trading wine with Bordeaux and port with Oporto, it follows that there should be an excellent vintners in Dartmouth. Hugh Heywood, recently retired owner of the Dartmouth Vintners, built up an extensive range of wines, spirits and beers in his shop on the corner of The Butterwalk. Wines here are nearly all from small independent producers. Staff at Dartmouth Vintners enjoy discussing needs with their customers, from the 'under a fiver' wine for the Sunday roast, to the finer details of malt whiskies, over eighty of which form part of a vast collection of miniatures. Local brews are also well supported, with Sharpham wines, Crannacombe cider, Bramley and Gage liqueurs and Blackawton

beer being just some of the South Hams produce on sale. When asked about his favourite tipple, Hugh Heywood suggested Quinta da Eira Velha—a vintage port from a Portuguese quinta owned by the Newman family, who own and still live at Blackpool Sands. There's an original bottle of Newman's port exhibited upstairs in the museum. And if you're looking for a good Bordeaux, try the red Le Voyageur 1994. **Dartmouth Vintners, 6 Duke Street,** ☎ 01803 832602.

Cliff's Cabin—The Dartmouth Tobacconist
Aniseed, lemon grove, honey menthol, and Irish coffee are just some of the flavours of snuff which can be bought at Cliff's Cabin, which also has an astonishing collection of pipes and lighters, not to mention the loose tobaccos and magnificently packaged rolling tobaccos including one 'Kentucky bird'—a mix of tobacco and flower petals. One of the few traditional tobacconists left in the country. **Cliff's Cabin, 12 Foss Street.**

Bags & buckets:
The Canvas Factory
Doug Briscoe, from Georgia USA, chartered his 60-foot yacht for some

Dartmouth

years, firstly around the Caribbean and later from Dartmouth. On board he had a sewing machine, which he used to repair sails and awnings. After circumnavigating the globe in 1994–95 he sold the boat, but kept the sewing machine. Those were the beginnings of The Canvas Factory, which he opened in Foss Street in July 1996. Using 15–18oz Indian canvas, Doug Briscoe constructs containers of all shapes and sizes,working from traditional patterns: the classic American ice bag, for example, forms the basis of The Canvas Factory shopping bag; and a horse's nose bag is the inspiration behind (surprise!) their Nose Bag. From the pencil cases, spectacle bags, and baby buckets, to vast grip bags, cruising bags, laundry buckets, even sturdy canvas shelves, The Canvas Factory manages to make things which are absolutely functional as well as being wonderful

objects in their own right. Goods are available by mail order, or (costing a little less) at **The Canvas Factory, 5 Foss Street ☎ 01803 832186.**

Craft
The town has no fewer than three Craft Council registered galleries: Facets, which exhibits and sells a diverse selection of

contemporary jewellery, Simon Drew (of whom more later), and the Higher Street Gallery, where there's glassware ceramics, turned wood, and jewellery by a range of fine craftsmen and women. **Facets, 14 Broadstone ☎ 01803 833534. Simon Drew Gallery, 13 Foss St ☎ 01803 832832. Higher Street Gallery, 1 Higher Street 0183 833157.**

Galleries
Simon Drew's witty pen and ink work has found its way onto mugs, teacloths and T-shirts in his gallery

in Foss Street. There is a serious side to his work, which he exhibits on occasions with four other artists: John Gillo, Paul Riley, Andreas Kaldor and John Donaldson. Together they make up the Dartmouth 5. This posse of talented and contrasting artists occasionally team up for joint showings in the town. Art Week at the end of May provides an annual focus for the artistic community, with lots of events and shows buzzing in the Dartmouth galleries. **Andreas Kaldor Gallery, 15 Newcomen Road ☎ 01803 833874. The Potting Shed, 12 Newcomen Road ☎ 01803 833591. D'Art Gallery, 4 Lower Street ☎ 01803 834923. John Gillo Gallery, Old Market Square ☎ 01803 833833. Foss Street Galleries, 17 Foss Street ☎ 01803 834311.**

Cliff and Val Mason of Cliff's Cabin / Doug Briscoe of The Canvas Factory / Simon Drew and his dog

Dartmouth

Food

It could be due to the huge success and high standards of the hallowed and heavenly **Carved Angel** that there is now a wealth of good eating places in Dartmouth. Even the simple sandwich has a place.

The Crabshell is a tiny kiosk tucked away in Raleigh Street, which runs between Newcomen Road (named after Thomas Newcomen, who erected the first successful steam engine in 1712—there is a small museum dedicated to Newcomen adjoining the Tourist Information building) and Lower Street. It serves seafood sandwiches. There is one choice of bread—the freshest of light wholemeal. This is filled with one of four choices: salmon, smoked mackerel, prawn, or fresh dill-baked salmon. No frisée lettuce garnish, no irritating crisps on the side of the plate. A terrific formula. Knockout sandwiches, at low prices. **Crabshell Seafoods, Raleigh Street ☎ 01803 835351.**

The Singing Kettle

This small café serves a mean home-made junket, amongst a menu of scrumptious boy's favourite school puddings. Cook Debbie Morris makes these enduring puddings as well as fresh springy and delicious cakes. The Devon apple cake and carrot cake disappear very rapidly, I'm told. Tucked away from the main drag, The Singing Kettle attracts local custom, and keeps prices down. **The Singing Kettle, 6 Smith Street ☎ 01803 832624. Open Tuesday to Sunday 10–5.**

For those who missed breakfast or just want another one, it has to be a trip to **Alf Resco's.** This busy warehouse café hangs loose—at last, relaxed café culture hits the South-West. Here families can eat and drink together or sit around reading newspapers and drinking coffee. Alf Resco's extended breakfasts are served from 10–2.30, Wednesday through Sunday. Try scrambled eggs with smoked salmon, or baguettes packed with salami or mozzarella and tomato. And as the name suggests, there is a vine-shaded terrace with a flaming torch over the archway where we can pretend the sun shines. **Café Alf Resco, Lower Street ☎ 01803 835880.**

The Carved Angel Café

offers a chance to get a taste of Joyce Molyneux's recipes (about which many have heard, and fewer have tried) for a fraction of

the cost of eating at the restaurant. **The Carved Angel Café, 7 Foss Street ☎ 01803 834842.**

Dartmouth is an unlikely place to come across a Venezuelan restaurant. **Aragua,** tucked away behind St Saviour's church, is the place to go for a very special occasion. The restaurant presents a series of sensual discoveries, from the weight and feel of the wine glasses and the crispness of the linen, to the explosive canapés and petit fours. Amongst these rather formal and austere surroundings burst hot latinate paintings. Food here is cooked with a passion, and presented exquisitely within these whitewashed walls. **Aragua Restaurant, St Saviour's Square, Anzac Street ☎ 01803 832224.**

Alf Resco's

Dartmouth

Two Hotels
An inn since 1736, and host to numerous distinguished guests, including the original Siamese twins, Chang and Eng, who lived joined at the hip till they were sixty-four, it would be easy to dwell upon the heritage of such a venerable institution as the **Royal Castle Hotel**. The present owner, Nigel Way, however, looks to the future. What at first sight seems a busy but fairly traditionally run hotel, is nothing of the sort. For Mr Way and his staff have put into action the greenest of working practices. Low energy light bulbs, refillable jars, and jugs of milk (no nasty cartons), bicycles for hire, recycling and buying locally are all the order of the day. When guests arrive at the Royal Castle, their cars are valet parked—a polite way of saying that they are taken away from them. Mr Way then seizes his moment and presents the (now carless) visitor with a pamphlet of suggestions of places to go and things to do without a car in and around Dartmouth. From a self-guided walk about town to more ambitious itineraries of 'boat there, train back' trips to Totnes. Excuses like 'I haven't got a bicycle' hold about as much water as his low-flush loos. The Hotel is happy to provide these—bicycles, that is—along with backpacks and packed lunches. **Royal Castle Hotel, The Quay** ☎ 01803 833033.

The Gunfield Hotel is reputed to have been built by French prisoners during the Napoleonic wars. This villa occupies a prime site built into the cliff close to Dartmouth Castle. Views from the hotel terrace northwards flow up the Dart, taking in the sweep of Dartmouth itself; southwards, they look out to sea.

Owned (and considerably revamped) by Mike and Lucy Swash, the place has a light, easy style to it. Amongst the ochres and umber washed walls are Paul Riley's sun-filled watercolours, and Zoe Oxenbury's mural makes for an absorbing trip to the loo. Underwoodsman Jason Griffiths has hewn the bar from a crooked oak found on Dartmoor, and the mirror frame from burr oak. On a lower terrace outside, a spacious deck for summer evening barbecues has been carefully constructed—for landscaping projects hereabouts have their hazards. 'One Gun', the site of the hotel, was once a burial ground for those who died on board visiting ships—a neighbour stumbled across four human lower mandibles whilst shifting her borders. Food in the restaurant is mediterranean and unfussy, with prices, fortunately, not as staggering as the views. **The Gunfield Hotel, Castle Road** ☎ 01803 834571.

Trips out from Dartmouth

An off-peak visit to **Dartmouth** is recommended, for in the high season the centre of town can be a nightmare. Trippers tumble out of coaches on to the embankment in their droves. However it's not difficult to shed the crowds pretty quickly if you head towards the edges of the town. Here are some suggestions:

The Walks The first of these is to Old Mill Creek, the first creek upstream from Dartmouth. The walk takes in the church at Townstal, and descends into the quiet of this lovely creek, where many of the Dartmouth boats are repaired. Warfleet is the second outing: this takes in the Dartmouth castle and the pottery. Then it's over the river to Kingswear by ferry for the third outing, a fairly strenuous walk which goes as far as the National Trust Gardens of Coleton Fishacre. There is an option to return to Kingswear along the coastal path.

Walk 1: Old Mill Creek A short way up river from Dartmouth on the west bank is Old Mill Creek. As it is not possible at the time of writing to take a flat route along the water's edge from the town, because of restricted MoD property, we follow the first leg of the Dartmouth to Dittisham part of the Dart Valley Trail, up to Townstal. To get there, at the end of Foss Street, turn left up Browns Hill Steps. From Browns Hill, turn left uphill along Clarence Hill. Cross Victoria Road and walk up Church Road to Townstal Church.

The church is the oldest in Dartmouth, and is approached by a yew-studded pathway through the graveyard. Over the years, movement in the ground has shifted the stones into a disorderly gathering, studded with angels, chains and anchors.

From the church, cross the main road (College Way) into Old Mill Road. This steeply winding road leads down to the head of Old Mill

On the ferry to Kingswear / A mariner's grave in Townstal churchyard

Creek. A single house, and boat sheds for maintenance and repair, are the only buildings in the creek. At low tide, it is empty of boats save for a few discarded vessels. The foreshore is busy with gulls, herons and redshanks feeding in the mud. In the summer, common and arctic terns can be seen here, and occasionally black terns visit. From here it is possible to take a permissive path along the northern shore which is close to the water's edge, or continue the walk along the public footpath to Dittisham as outlined in the Dart Valley Trail.

From the Water A visit by water is recommended: Old Mill Creek is accessible for one and a half hours either side of high tide. On the southern side of the bank on the foreshore at Sandquay Woods is Hermitage Castle. This extraordinary structure is built into the steep bank beside the water's edge. Entered from a grassy clearing in the woods above, steps descend into deepening darkness, finally arriving at shore level. Sadly, the building is in such disrepair that it is now unsafe to enter. Probably built around 1800, ladies no doubt passed the time there sewing stumpwork or painting watercolours, even taking a dip in the waters from the earthy bathing house below. The castle is just one of many remnants of the Raleigh Estate, upon which the Royal Naval College is now built.

A pleasure garden, and a grotto fashioned from moss lichen and tree stumps, which may well have supported its own resident hermit, were also part of what was known as Mount Boone. In the mud at Hermitage Creek lie the bulky remains of an

SOCKS THAT STARTLE

Several years ago, little egrets were a rare sight on the estuary. Now these smaller all-white versions of herons, more usually found in France and further south, have made their home here. Their bright yellow legs give a clue to their strange method of fishing: waving their legs around in the shallows to startle the fish, which momentarily stop in their tracks, giving the little egret the opportunity to seize the fish with his beak.

Old Mill Creek

GURGLY JUG

A dubious connection with the Newfoundland cod trade is the 'gurgel krug', 'pichet glou glou' or 'jarro gorgoteante', sold widely as a souvenir in the 1960s and 1970s. It's a jug in the body of a curled-tailed cod, which, when water is poured through its gaping mouth, produces deep gurgly sounds. Margaret Thatcher, when presented with one in 1978, thought it would go 'very well with the decorations at Downing Street'.

old Colchester barge, with grass growing from its hull like cress in an eggshell. Further out in the creek on a mudbank is the wreck of the Irish sailing coaster 'Invermore' of Castleford. The wreck of the Spanish galleon 'Madre de Dios' is also thought to be somewhere in the creek. After it was captured from the tail end of the Armada fleet, the ship had been brought into Dartmouth and used as a hospital ship, most probably in Old Mill Creek. A whale was washed up in Old Mill Creek in 1865, and more recently a school of confused porpoises became marooned in its waters. More contemporary itinerants found their way to the Creek in the eighties, when a group of Irish houseboat dwellers moored up there for a spell. It is a romantic and intriguing place.

Walk 2: Warfleet

Easily overlooked, Warfleet is a quiet creekside community tucked beneath the road which leads to the Dartmouth Pottery. Sketched by the painter J.M.W. Turner on a visit to Devon in 1811, this quiet inlet remains a community apart. It has escaped prettying up and labelling, and long may it remain thus. An elderly resident swims daily in the creek, on the shores of which lime kilns are returning gently to the earth. Close by is the Boat House, which stands on the pebble beach, available for holiday lets. This has the sure sniff of adventure. Warfleet is easily walked to from town via the Newcomen Road. At the viaduct, take the path which leads down to Warfleet.

Further up the road is the **Dartmouth Pottery** and factory shop, a rare example of industrial architecture in Dartmouth. The Pottery is housed in the old Paper Mills at Warfleet. Mills have been in existence on this site since the mid-seventeenth century. Over the main entrance across the footbridge are the letters 'A.H.H.', the initials of Dartmouth entrepreneur and landowner Arthur H. Holdsworth. The Mill, once powered by a mammoth water-wheel fifty feet in diameter, produced a high quality paper from coloured cotton rags. The paper was used, amongst other things, for the local Dartmouth banknotes: a £1 note survives in the town museum. Subsequently, the mills produced flour and, after the wheel had been used for firewood, it became a brewery producing firstly 'Barley Wine from the English Rhine', then 'Warfleet Pale Ales—the finest beer in Britain', using the pure water from the valley stream for washing bottles and for the beer itself. Mud from the mill pond fed the market garden alongside it, which grew soft fruits and vegetables, and later watercress. After years of lying empty, commandos used the building as their headquarters during World War II, and in 1948 it became a pottery.

Dartmouth Pottery has a tradition of embracing all tastes. In the 1950s and 1960s it produced 'Polka Dot' ware, 'Cottage' ware and the hugely popular 'Motto' ware. Collectors of pottery are advised to scour the local charity shops and jumble sales for it.

In the 1960s, the Dartmouth Pottery brought out its 'TV Set'—a rectangular plate with circular lip for steadying the mug which stood upon it, enabling the viewer to follow the plot without the distraction of having to cope with cup, saucer and plate independently. The present owners are Samuel Heath Ltd, whose products still manage to embrace many tastes. From lumpish pink piggy banks to the exuberant Rainbow Ware of Marjya Boxer: in the shape of hearts, petals, diamonds and squares, in a range of strong colours, and spied in the finest of London restaurants. Seconds can be picked up in the Pottery shop from this and other ranges, and a coffee shop makes a welcome stop off after browsing. **Dartmouth Pottery, Warfleet ☎ 01803 833486.**

The Castle and Beyond

From Warfleet you can wander along the road, which will take you to Dartmouth Castle. Alternatively, there is a small passenger ferry from Bayard's Cove to Dartmouth Castle.

Boat rides for small children can be an adventure—for about five minutes. An ideal trip for those with little ones is to the castle from the town. The experience of being in a small boat and seeing Dartmouth from the water,

WARFLEET KILNS

In the nineteenth century, itinerants and local children were attracted by the warmth of a working lime kiln. The unfortunate Henry Avis, aged 12, was burnt to death at the Warfleet kilns when he accidentally fell asleep and rolled into the burning kiln. By all accounts he was a lonely boy, who lived with his grandfather at the baths near the castle. *(See box on page 109 for a further note on lime kilns.)*

ST PETROX

Petrox is the mediæval mis-spelling of Petroc, a sixth-century missionary and aesthete to whom the church is dedicated. Given to eating ashes and reciting the psalter up to his waist in the Camel Estuary, Petroc journeyed widely—to Rome, Jerusalem, the Indian Ocean, Wales, Brittany and Devon, spreading the relatively hot news of Christianity. Between trips, he retreated to his hermitage cell in Padstow. After his death on June 4th 564, his relics (true to form) proved somewhat itinerant, being snatched back and forth between assorted Celtic resting places. Eventually they were lost somewhere between Bodmin and Brittany. The cask, however, empty of relics, was finally recovered last century and enshrined with dignity at St Petroc's Church, Bodmin.

albeit briefly, is a delightful and inexpensive one. At the castle end there are a lot of steps to climb, but once at the top the excuse to pause is the church of **St Petrox**: spare and bleak in its simplicity, and exposed to the brunt of the weather. The earliest record of a place of worship on this site predates the Norman conquest. It's a sobering place, suited to reflection and prayer. Should you wish to attend a service, evensong is nightly at 6.30.

Dartmouth Castle   Hewn from, and into, the rock face at the mouth of the estuary, the castle is just one of four defences built on the site to protect Dartmouth from attackers. Building started in 1481 by order of Edward IV, and the castle was completed by 1494. The first in the country to be designed for artillery, guns were placed in the basement near the waterline, while the soldiers were accommodated in the floors above. At times of threat, a chain was stretched across the water to Gomerock, close to Kingswear Castle which stands on the opposite bank. Now and then, vivid re-enactments are staged around the defences: groups set up camp, living, working, fighting, eating and dressing in fifteenth-century style. The Castle is a tremendous setting for such an event, and young audiences love it. **Dartmouth Castle ☎ 01803 833588.**

Coastward from the Castle   Dartmouth Castle is worth noting for its woodland and coastal walks alone. An information board in the castle car park shows four easy waymarked trails to follow. These include walks to Gallants Bower, where earth banks are all that remain of a royalist fort; and a walk to Sugary Cove, with steps leading down to the beach. A walk to the Coastguard's Cottages along the springy grass and heathland is strewn with sea kale in the early summer, and an excellent source of sloe berries in the autumn.

Notes on the coast

Castle Cove was once lined with coloured beach huts and diving boards. Traditionally it was a place where Dartmouth children learned to swim. The public baths were also nearby. A little further round the coast is Ladies Cove which, as its name suggests, was reserved for ladies' swimming only. Each season, bathing machines were floated round to the cove, where they were used for transporting delicate Victorian ladies into the restorative waters without risking an unseemly exposure of flesh.

Compass Point: A lookout point since the year dot: in the early 1600s, a compass and watch house were built here, 'to discern and try the winds and keep the sea watch as in ancient time hath been accustomed'.

Warren Point: Rabbits were a thirteenth-century introduction to Britain from Italy. Rabbit husbanders didn't know the half of it when they set about the practice of commercial rabbit breeding. A commercial rabbit warren was registered here at Warren Point in 1613. Rabbits were bred for their meat and fur; they were kept in pillow mounds, and granite vermin traps were set for unfortunate predators.

THE SLOE

or Blackthorn tree or 'Wild Plum of Western Europe' has a small round blackish fruit, with green acid-flavoured flesh. The tree 'has no value except for making sloe wine and sloe gin' according to the Oxford book of Food Plants. Sloe gin is valued highly by the many who make and drink it during the winter moths.

For sloe gin, pick sloes in winter after the first frosts. They should be plump and a dull purplish black. Take them home and wash them, then either prick each sloe with a pin several times—or cheat, and put them in the freezer overnight then defrost (but they don't look quite so good in the bottle this way).

Measure out 12 oz white sugar to each pound of sloes, and put in a wide mouthed jar. Top up with a pint of gin. Put in a cool place, and up-end the jar occasionally to dissolve the sugar. Ready for drinking in about two to three months, but tastes better when kept for a year or more. Sloe gin is a dark carmine colour, and has a rich warming flavour.

Walk 3: Bramble Jelly and Beyond

A coastal walk from Kingswear to Coleton Fishacre. A pound for the ferry, and a couple more for preserves, should cover the cost of this trip discovering the coastal area around Kingswear.

Take the Lower Ferry from near Bayard's Cove to Kingswear. First

follow the coastal path 'acorn' sign, then take the route under the archway opposite The Royal Dart Hotel, and climb up Alma Steps. Note the small garden reserved for the use of the elderly of the parish. Once on Beacon Road, houses, plants and vistas begin to grow larger. Here in late summer *Agapanthus* grow to massive proportions amongst the generous fans and spires of other subtropical plants.

On the seaward side of the road, astonishingly steep gardens descend the cliffs, obscuring views of the estuary mouth below. Close by, at the water's edge, is Kingswear Castle, the location of which is so exposed to salt and water that the original iron guns corroded and had to be replaced with brass ones. The Castle itself is available for rent through the Landmark Trust—for that elemental break! On the hill above is another fortification, Fort Ridley, which last saw action during the Civil War.

Veering a little away from the coast, the lane becomes short and steep and barely wide enough for one person. Rocky Lane follows the line of a spring. It is along here, in a pretty wooden shelter, that jars of homemade preserves may be on sale. Depending on season, it may be bramble jelly, a more exotic peach or plum preserve, even fruit butters such as organic Lemon Butter with Elderflower. Jars cost between £1.75 and £2.50.

Carry on up the lane, past Brownstone car park on the right and on to **Coleton Fishacre**, the landscaped gardens and house of the D'Oyly Carte family—of Sadler's Wells and Gilbert and Sullivan fame. The house has only recently been opened to the public. To enjoy this National Trust property to the full, you will need plenty of reserves of energy, for this plantsman's garden, developed over the years between 1926–47 by Rupert and Dorothy D'Oyly Carte, covers acres of steeply wooded ground and supports a

Lomatia ferrunginea AT COLETON FISHACRE

This evergreen foliage plant, a native of rainforests of Chile and Patagonia, was introduced to this country through William Lobb at Veitch's nursery in Exeter. A very rare specimen was discovered at Coleton Fishacre when the National Trust took it on in 1983, as were many other rarities, including the Australian tea tree.

Milestone at Kingswear

AUTUMN HEDGE TREATS

When walking in the autumn, remember to take a bag to fill with berries and nuts. Early autumn treats will include the obvious blackberries—and the less picked elderberries (delicious stewed with apples or turned into wild Ribena—see below). Later in the season, green hazelnuts are delicious from their shells, ripe rosehips, rowans and haws from prickly hawthorn bushes, and sloes as already mentioned earlier. Leave some berries to see the birds through the colder months. Try making jam or cordial to enjoy in deepest winter.

HEDGEROW JELLY

Pick a quantity of each of the following: elderberries, rosehips, blackberries, sloes and crab apples. Exact proportions are not that important—but don't let one dominate or it will mask the other flavours. Rinse the fruits well and chop the crab apples. Put into a large pan with a base covering of water. Cook well until soft, then mash with a potato masher to form a thick pulp. Strain the pulp through a jelly bag or muslin tied to the legs of an upturned stool. Leave overnight to drip. Measure the resulting juice. Put in a large pan with 1 lb white granulated sugar to every

pint of juice. Stir until the sugar has dissolved then boil rapidly until set point has been reached (104 degrees on a jam thermometer—or put a little on a cold saucer in the fridge and see if a skin forms on it). Put into warm sterilised jars (under a low grill or 2 minutes in microwave for 6 jars), cover when still hot and label. NB: consider where you pick your fruits—'wild' does not equal 'organic'.

ELDERBERRY CORDIAL

Strip berries off the stems and place in a large pan with a little water to simmer (stainless steel if possible). When the berries are reduced to a juice, strain the resulting purple liquid and add 8oz white sugar to each pint of juice. Simmer again for a few minutes to dissolve (but not to cook like jam). Pour into clean glass bottles with screw top lids. The cordial will keep for months in a cool dark place. It is full of vitamin C. Dilute with hot or cold water as with Ribena.

BLACKBERRY JAM

Remove stalks wash and drain fruit. Crush the fruit and bring slowly to the boil, stirring continuously. Add 3/4 lb sugar to each pound of fruit and boil till set; 30–40 minutes. Pour into clean dry jars and seal.

wide range of tender and uncommon trees. It is perhaps at its best in springtime, when the camellias, rhododendrons and magnolias are in full force. A reviver in the pretty tea garden is recommended before setting out on the return journey. A military road leads past the lime-stone day beacon, which has served as a navigational point for boats since the 1870s. There follows a muscle-toning stretch as the coastal path is rejoined for the last leg back to the village of Kingswear. **Coleton Fishacre, Brownstone, Kingswear ☎ 01803 752466.**

Dittisham

The Lord's my Shepherd, I'll not want,
He maketh me down to lie.
In pastures green
He leadeth me
The quiet waters by.
[Written by Rev. Francis Rous,
born in Dittisham c.1600]

Dittisham is built around a promontory three miles upstream from Dartmouth. Houses tumble down the hill to a rocky waterfront, where lines of boats flap around the pier and jetty. The village stands on a bend in the river, close to a stretch of water known as the Dittisham Lake, where at high tide the river is almost a mile across to Galmpton on the far shore. Such a wondrous setting has led to houses being acquired by the very rich, many being used for second homes. Local families have had to retreat to the more affordable margins of the village.

The Domesday survey records the village as Didashim—meaning homestead of Deedas, who was thought to have been a Saxon leader around 660 AD. The Black Death, which was first reported in Devon in 1349, struck Dittisham very hard,

Ray Humphreys, Dart Estuary Officer

and large numbers of victims were buried there—Dittisham has had a burial ground for at least a thousand years, with around 18,000 people believed to be interred around the parish. From the ancient church of St George at Dittisham there are far-reaching views of the river and surrounding countryside, and beside the church are some of the oldest cottages in the village. Dittisham has some fine exam-

PINK COTTAGES

Note the traditional pink painted cottages in and around Dittisham. To achieve this pink, lime was mixed to a 'milk' with water to make limewash A popular way to colour it was to mix in ox blood, which turned the wash a delightful shade of pink, now much imitated by the paint manufacturers and used for thatched cottages everywhere.

ples of traditional local architecture, with stone and cob cottages beneath thatched or local slate rooves. Elderly stone walls hung with gardens of wildflowers, and ancient hedgerows, flank the snaking village lanes.

In spring, Dittisham was once buried beneath blossom which foamed from the many plum and damson orchards. The village even had its own species of plum, thought to have been introduced to the village by visiting German sailors. Sadly, many of those orchards have been grubbed up, but in late July the few trees which survive still produce fruit, which can be seen for sale in baskets on the occasional doorstep.

Whether crabbing from the jetty, pausing for a drink at the Ferry Boat Inn, or simply waiting for the foot ferry, the quay is a perfect place to idle away the time. The water bubbles with activity. Dittisham has its own yacht club, sailing school and annual regatta, which is held at the end of

July or beginning of August. The Ham car park has direct access to the water for launching small craft. At the top of the village is the **Red Lion Inn**. This pub, favoured by the locals, has a good children's room and is very popular for Sunday lunches. The village shop is well stocked for everyday needs, and also sells a good selection of local produce. **The Red Lion Inn, The Level, Dittisham ☎ 01803 722235.**

The Ferry Boat Inn, on the river front, is a good stopping place for winter walkers. It has a lovely open fire, spectacular views, and serves large and oozy brie and mushroom

The Ferry Inn

DATING A HEDGE

Hedges can be hundreds, sometimes thousands of years old. If you are passing a thick hedge which appears to have a mixture of trees and shrubs in it, you can try to age it by the following method. It sounds quite *ad hoc*, but it can be surprisingly accurate:

Lay a stick down at one point along the hedge and walk 30 wide paces away. As you retrace your steps, count the number of different species of trees and woody shrubs in your stretch of the hedge. Trees may include ash, beech, rowan, pine etc. Shrubs could include dogwood, hawthorn, blackthorn, elder, hazel, holly etc., but not climbing plants such as rose, honeysuckle or ivy. The number of species generally corresponds to a century. So if there are seven different species, the hedge is around seven hundred years old.

baguettes at lunchtime. **The Ferry Boat Inn, Manor Street, Dittisham ☎ 01803 722368.**

The Dittisham and Cornworthy area is laced with craftspeople of one sort or another. Beavering away in their homes and workshops, it is only on occasions that their work becomes visible. An annual craft fair takes place before Christmas, at which the standard of work is exceptionally high. Keep an eye on the noticeboards for such events or exhibitions.

Bridget McCrum's Garden Dittisham is the home of sculptor Bridget McCrum. For two weekends in May, her riverside garden is open to the public as part of the National Gardens Scheme. The sculptures are an integral part of this garden, which is more to do with uplifting walks and enjoyment of space and form than drifts of flowers.

Greenway Gardens Nursery A perfect excuse to cross the river by foot ferry is the plant nursery at Greenway on the east bank of the Dart. Roger Clarke, who runs this specialist nursery, is also in charge of the exceptional riverside gardens at Greenway. Once the house of Agatha Christie, it is now lived in by her daughter. Greenway's spectacular gardens were established at the turn of the century by the Williams family, who were well-known plant collectors. The garden is filled with trees and shrubs from their time there: magnificent specimens grace this garden, which opens to the public for two to three days in March and April in time to catch the tulip trees and other early spring shrubs in flower. Roger Clarke has personally developed the garden during recent

Maypool, Greenway

years, specialising in specimens from the southern hemisphere, in particular plants from Chile, New Zealand and South Africa. Cuttings and seeds from these and other plants at Greenway are sold in the nursery. At the time of writing, the National Trust are in the process of acquiring the Gardens, so they will soon be open to the public on a permanent basis. The Nursery is open all year round: 2.00–5.00 pm Monday to Friday (4.30 pm in the winter months), and 10.00–12.00 am Saturday mornings. The ferry may be summoned by ringing the bell on the wall beside the Ferry Inn (or ☎ 01803 844010). Directions: from the ferry landing stage on the Greenway side, walk up the hill. Three hundred metres up the lane on the right is a five-bar gate. Turn right there: this lane is a short cut to Greenway Nursery. **Greenway Gardens Nursery ☎ 01803 842382.**

Cornworthy

The village of Cornworthy is almost lost between the hills that surround it. The dark stone buildings give it a rather serious air (stone quarried from Cornworthy was used in the building of Dartmouth Castle). It still has the atmosphere of a working village, and although it recently lost its shop, the pub—the **Hunters Lodge Inn**—is very much alive. Outside the church of St Peter is a splendid old oak tree; inside is the parish book, which allows the visitor a privileged insight into the village. A leaflet has also been produced which details waymarked circular walks in the parish. [The Circular Walk Pamphlet costs 25p; available in the Hunters Lodge Inn and the Church.]

Cornworthy Priory In a field a quarter of a mile to the west of the village stands the remains of the double-entranced gatehouse of Cornworthy Priory. Mounds in the surrounding fields mark where its walls once stood. Dedicated to St Mary, the priory was

FROM CRADLE TO COFFIN

The most we collect from a hedgerow now is probably a few blackberries in Autumn. Years ago, many farm labourers were 'given' a length of hedge to manage and use—hence the hedges were kept in good repair. In laying a hedge you could take out firewood, coppice ash and hazel, cut lengths for tool handles, and let a few mature trees grow for your old age. When cut, they would provide saleable timber, some wood to carve for furniture—for a grandchild's cradle or for your own coffin.

founded for a small community of Augus-
tinian nuns around 1230. Records of the
priory are fragmented, but by 1461 it seems
the nuns had become a little slack in their
religious observations. An admonitory letter
from Bishop John Vesey at his Chudleigh
palace to the Prioress Avis Dynham implies
that life at the Priory must have become far
too secular. He instructed them henceforth
not to dress in pompous apparel, to sleep in
the one dormitory and to eat together,
listening to the 'complative lectour', to refrain from meddling in outside
husbandry and wandering in the fields and other profane places. They
were forbidden to receive sojourners, and were to remove within one
month all the servants not necessary for the place.

Fifteen years later, Henry VIII's commissioners arrived to assess the
value of the convent's possessions; the dissolution of all the religious
houses was complete by 1539. Pinned to the gate beside the ruin is a hand-
painted sign directing the visitor to the source of Priory spring water.

Carpenter Oak is an architectural service based in East Cornworthy,
which specialises in crucked oak barn structures, built in the traditional
manner by a team of skilled carpenters. Along the road between
Dittisham and Cornworthy, two Carpenter Oak buildings are visible: one
is at Lamper Head, on high ground above the river, and another can be
seen close by Dittisham Mill Creek (the home of kingfishers). These are
very successful examples of 'bungalow eating', whereby the oak additions
have devoured an unremarkable bungalow bit by bit, transforming it into
a building of architectural merit. **Carpenter Oak and Woodland Ltd,
Longlands Workshop, East Cornworthy
☎ 01803 732900.**

Produce, Crafts and Makers

Between East Cornworthy and
Dittisham, in the village of Capton, is
the workshop of blacksmith **John
Churchill**, who produces handmade
architectural and domestic ironmon-
gery. A visit is strongly recommended.
His unfussy collection of latches,

Dittisham Mill Creek / Carpenter Oak building

catches, vanes, poles, stays, hooks and handles are a breath of fresh air. John Churchill's commissions have included weathervanes, gates, staircases and metal stepping stones. Visit by appointment. **John Churchill, The New Forge, Capton ☎ 01803 712276.**

Tideford Foods make fresh soups and sauces cooked from seasonal ingredients and hermetically sealed in chunky glass jars. They offer four seasonal menus: Spring includes watercress sauce, crab and mango soup, and lamb and flageolet cassoulet; Autumn, parsnip and ginger soup and confit de canard, salsa verde and walnut sauce. Tideford pesto is reliably good with pasta. Contact them for details of nearby stockists, or you can buy direct from them by mail order. **Tideford Foods, Higher Tideford Farm, Cornworthy ☎ 01803 712276.**

Whitestone Cider Company 'Old Pig Squeal' cider has been produced traditionally at Riverside Farm, East Cornworthy, since 1989. Still, natural apple juice is also made on the premises. **Whitestone Cider ☎ 01803 722400.**

Dittisham Sailing School Two-hour sailing lessons on Wayfarers, learn from scratch or brush up your helming. **Sunny Bank, Manor Street, Dittisham ☎ 01803 722375.**

Coombe Farm Studios Paul and Tina Riley have run art and

DEVON'S DEEP LANES

The first thing that will strike you about South Devon is the deep and narrow hedged lanes, which twist and turn. Not built for cars, Devon lanes were made by and for packhorses, and by respecting everyone's landholding, they got travellers from A to B in a rather roundabout way.

On narrow 'green lanes' that haven't been widened for cars, you can still see the ridges in the hedgebanks made by generations of wooden pack saddles forcing their way through. With no surfacing, heavy winter rain and fertile soils, these lanes became pools of mud, and had to be regularly scraped back to a harder surface (the mud being dumped on either side), thus creating or deepening the 'Devon banks'. In coastal areas, these deep lanes had their own advantages, and the locals made them deeper still—to hide the packhorses, and people carrying smuggled goods, from the customs men.

The ridge roads—for example the road that runs from the coast near Slapton past East Allington, through Moreleigh, Diptford and onto the south side of Dartmoor—were used for driving sheep up onto moorland grazing for the summer months. Young men would stay with the flocks on the moor for perhaps three or four months before returning to winter in the sheltered valleys of the South Hams.

craft courses from Coombe since 1982. The converted stone barns assembled round a courtyard provide a wonderful environment for living and working. There is also an exhibition space which shows work by makers, predominantly from the Westcountry. Paul Riley's vibrant and accomplished watercolours are an inspiration to any student. Other courses run here include pottery, papier maché, printmaking, jewellery

and indigo dyeing. Friends and family may accompany students on a bed and breakfast basis, and group bookings are welcomed. **Coombe Farm Studios, Dittisham ☎ 01803 722352. Gallery open Mon–Sat 10am–5pm.**

Fingals Being a guest at Fingals is a bit like dropping in on a house-party. Meals are lengthy, sociable affairs, in which a restricted choice of dishes ensures absolute freshness. Fingals welcomes casual walkers for a cup of tea or a drink. There is an ease about the place, which is scattered with generous flourishes from the owners Richard and Sheila Johnston, who somehow manage to give the impression that running such a fabulous spread is quite without effort. **Fingals, Old Coombe Manor Farm, Dittisham ☎ 01803 722398.**

STRONGEST PAPER IN THE WORLD

A paper expert collector and enthusiast—a Mr Dalhunter of Ohio, ordered fifteen rolls of Tuckenhay paper for papering the walls of his house, for he believed it to be the strongest paper in the world. It was also used for mourning notepaper on the death of George VI; Government of Siam Banknotes, and the pages of George V stamp albums.

Bow Creek

Up river from Dittisham is Bow Creek, which stretches for a mile until it reaches the village of **Tuckenhay**. Disused quays and warehouses are left as reminders of past trading from the village— cider was once shipped to London from here, as was stone for road-making. The village manufactured gas, which was used for lighting as early as 1806.

It also had two paper mills, one of which (Arthur Millbourn and Co) continued to make finest quality paper until the 1970s.

The Maltsters A fabulous situation beside the creek, a great ambience, and good food are three reasons to visit the Maltsters. It also has the plus of being hospitable to both dogs and children, for whom there is a menu (the children, that is) which for once doesn't assume under twelves to have palates of polystyrene. **The Maltsters Arms, Tuckenhay ☎ 01803 732350.**

Ashprington

Ashprington is a rather refined and sedate village set on a hill close to Sharpham House and Vineyard (see below).

Avenue Cottage Gardens Originally part of the 18th century land-scaped garden of Sharpham House, these eleven acres of garden and woodland are approached through a splendid avenue of turkey oaks which were planted in 1844. The present owners are busy recreating vistas and clearing overplanted areas for replanting. Teas by arrangement. Open end of March to beginning of October, Tues–Sat 11.00 am–5.00 pm. **Avenue Cottage Gardens, Ashprington ☎ 01803 732769.**

Sharpham Vineyard Whether walking along the river from Totnes, or dropping off by boat, a visit to the vineyards at Sharpham is a pleasant diversion. The vineyards and dairy form part of the estate, the home of Maurice Ash, son-in-law of the Elmhirsts of Dartington and for many years Chairman of the Dartington Hall Trust. Experiments in living continue at the Sharpham Community, where there is a College of Buddhist and Ecological Studies.

Occasional summer evening boat trips with music and food include a trip to the vineyard for cheese (from Sharpham Creamery) and wine tasting. Two self-guided trails have been made around the glorious 14-acre vineyard: the red, or vineyard trail, takes a circular route through the vines, whereas the blue trail follows the vineyard trail for the first part then takes a route beside the water's edge, finishing at the winery where tastings of the distinctive Sharpham wines may be arranged. **Sharpham Vineyard, Sharpham House, Ashprington ☎ 01803 732203** (please phone before visiting). **Sharpham Creamery, Ashprington ☎ 01803 732600.**

Sharpham Boathouse with Vineyard beyond

Totnes

The river remains navigable up to the weir at Totnes, where the first road bridge crosses the Dart.

A brief history

At a time when Vikings were paddling their way up every waterway in Devon, seizing who or whatever were in their way, Edward, elder son of Alfred the Great, was scouring the South Hams for sites to build his planned series of fortified towns as a defence against the ravages of the Danes. It was beside a fordable stretch of the River Dart near the main highway to Plymouth that Edward came across a steeply rising promontory. This he judged to be an ideal situation for one such town; plentiful fishing, fertile soil and and a fine lookout point at the top of the hill. Edward lost no time in calling in the King's men to build the walled town upon the hill which was named Totnes [*Tot* = lookout, and *ness* or *naise* = nose]. This was the early 900s. It is still possible to make out the original Saxon boat-shaped town of Totnes from the air, with tenements bordering the main street, and behind them long narrow garden strips (burgage plots) which stretched all the way to the town walls.

It was two hundred years later that Totnes Castle was built by Judhael—a Breton who had been given the town as a gift from William the Conqueror. He built the castle with forced labour, in so doing flattening the original settlement which had clustered upon the volcanic tip of the hill. Gradually, as the threat of invasion subsided, people risked building their homes closer and closer to the river Dart, which was the centre for trading cloth, leather and slate. It was cloth that became a major part of the town's economy; in 1253 'Totnes russet' had been chosen for the King's bed. The industry employed a

> ## A DEVONSHIRE DOZEN
>
> It was the practice in Devon to make cloth in its own peculiar dimensions: 12 yards long and one yard wide—a Devonshire Dozen.

large percentage of the Totnes work-
force—family names associated with the
cloth trade, such as Fuller, Tucker and
Dyer, are still common locally. Cloth
production went through many stages: by
the time the cloth reached the public space
where it was stretched on tenter hooks, it
had passed through the homes of both

spinners and weavers as well as the waterside tucking mills. The speed at
which the plague coursed through Totnes, wiping out two-thirds of the
town, was thought to be to do with the many hands the cloth passed
through during its manufacture.

By the 1500s, the Totnes merchants' overseas trade was flourishing.
The second richest town in Devon, Totnes was also benefitting from
trading in tin from Dartmoor. This rise in fortunes brought substantial
development to the town. A rash of new buildings sprang up, and
existing houses were fundamentally revamped to keep abreast of fashion.
By the end of the century there were as many as fifty new fashioned gable
houses with timber-framed oriel windows. The peak of Totnes's fortunes
was reached in the early 1600s, after which came a steady decline. By the
1700s the movers and shakers had moved on to more happening places,
leaving behind them a staid population remarkable only for its community of clockmakers. It had become little more than a rural market town,
a pleasant place to live, particularly for large families with small estates—
for produce was both abundant and cheap. Building had more or less
ceased with this decline in fortunes and it is thanks to the fact that Totnes

was never again so economically
buoyant that contemporary
Totnes is falling over itself in
superb examples of 16th and
17th century architecture with
all its attendant plasterwork,
courtyards and decorative slate
tiles. In fact, the town boasts the
highest incidence of listed
buildings per head of population in Britain.

Tudor houses of note in the
town can be found at 52 & 54

High Street, Totnes

High Street, 20 High Street, and 70 Fore Street (The Museum). Good examples of plasterwork are seen at 16 High Street (Nicholas Ball's house), 64 Fore Street, and the Council Chamber in the Guildhall.

Lesser notables of Totnes include Edward Lye, compiler of the first Anglo-Saxon Dictionary; and Benjamin Kennacot, compiler of the 'Hebrew Old Testament with various readings'.

Alternative Totnes—the Seeds

It was in the early 1800s when the first recorded attempt to put Totnes on the map as a centre for alternative health was made. A nameless entrepreneur made an attempt to market the medicinal waters from the Leech Wells. These waters, it was claimed, cured plague as well as curing skin disorders. Perhaps this was just an idea ahead of its time, for Totnes failed in its attempt to become a spa town and settled back into rural quiescence.

Entertainment

Diversions in the town took on various forms at different times. Bulls were baited on The Plains before and after church, and bowls were rolled on St Peter's Quay. Theatricals were played in assorted venues, including the theatre above No. 28 High Street, which might have also have served as a cockpit. The Totnes Races galloped on to the scene just before 1800, with large crowds gathering on the marshes to see the horses charge across the river and up into the farthest reaches of Bridgetown.

The coming of Dorothy and Leonard Elmhirst to Dartington in 1925 had a profound effect upon the locality. Leonard's ideal of creating a self-sufficient rural community, together with Dorothy's commitment to the arts, brought an injection of new energy to the area. Pioneers in all these fields visited or

Atherton Passage

worked in Dartington. Followers settled in neighbouring villages as well as in Totnes, in order to participate in what were undeniably exciting times. Before long, Totnes emerged as a thriving centre for alternative living. This has its advantages, for concentrated into the Totnes area is an extraordinary number of activities, businesses & events servicing the needs of alternative culture.

The Clock Tower from the High Street

Totnes

Art and Crafts

Totnes has a wealth of craftspeople living and working around the area: it would need a whole book to cover the subject properly. Some need seeking out, and others have outlets in local shops. A list of members of **The Devon Guild of Craftsmen** is available from their wonderful shop and exhibition centre at Bovey Tracey. **Devon Guild of Craftsmen, Riverside Mill, Bovey Tracey** ☎ **01626 832223.**

The craftspeople featured below reflect the huge and changing range of arts and crafts represented in the town. They are all in easy walking distance of each other.

Marshall Arts Work of members of the Devon Guild of Craftsmen may be seen in this small, vibrant gallery. Marshall Arts specialises in ceramics, including Rachel May's elegant lustre pottery in muted colours; Delam Cookson's characteristic blue vases, bowls and dishes; Mary Rich's exquisite intricately patterned porcelain work. Pat Keel Diffey's watercolours and etchings are also represented here, along with a fine range of other high quality work. **Marshall Arts, 2 Warland, The Plains** ☎ **01803 863533.** Open Tuesday to Saturday 10–1 and 2–5, closed Thursday afternoons.

Prismatic This craft co-operative sells high quality work by Devon's craftsmen and women. Turned wood by Chetan Raku, pottery by Desley White, sumptuous devouré scarves and clothes by Vicky King, and Jamie Inglis's understated jewellery, are just some of the works on sale in this tiny showroom. **Prismatic, 51 Fore Street**. Open Mon–Sat 10.00–5.00.

Fifth Element A great collection of jewellery can be seen here. If you want a very special ring, Trevor Forrester specialises in individually cast wedding rings, and he also makes delicate silver tiaras. In contrast, the bold colourful plastic jewellery of Jo Collam is remarkably inexpensive, considering the work involved. The hand-blown perfume bottles (with hand-ground stoppers) of Sark glassblower Tim Casey are delightful light-catching objects, in the richest of colours. **Fifth Element 3 Civic Hall Shops, Market Square** ☎ **01803 863191.** Open Fridays and Saturdays.

Number Seven—Toys For Collectors Houses the work of designers of automata (toys which move). Owner Vicki Wood made a working model of the defeat of the Spanish Armada, which is part of at the Drake exhibition at Buckland Abbey. You can find chomping alligators, rocking birds, drummers drumming, ladies dancing, and plenty more. **Number Seven, 7 High Street** ☎ **01803 866862.**

Shoes

Conker Shoes Conker's colourful wide-toed footwear has become almost a trademark for Totnes. Founded in the 1970s by Andy Langford, Conker Shoes now produces 150 pairs of handmade shoes per week, the materials for which are scrupulously resourced. Shoes can be bought by mail order. **Conker Shoe Co, 83 High Street** ☎ **01803 862490.**

Green Shoes Fine hand-made leather and vegan shoes produced by a

Isabel Forrester at Fifth Element

Totnes

company of women. Deeply comfortable, and particularly good for children's styles. Hilary Johnson's range of wonderfully practical yet elegant Ham bags are on sale in the shop. **Green Shoes, 69 High Street ☎ 01803 864997.**

Oliver Sweeney This Dartmoor-based shoemaker produces dress shoes and boots for men and women, available in **Diva** at the top of the High Street (which incidentally sells select lines in gorgeous quality women's clothes). For the very flush, Diva has opened another branch further down the road with designer outfits. **Diva, 55 High Street ☎ 01803 866681.**

Paper
Paperworks Sometimes humorous, and occasionally sumptuous, it's the fabulous papery displays in the window at

Paperworks which stop people in their tracks. The shop itself is a source of the gorgeous hand-made papers from India, Nepal, Thailand, Japan, and even Wookey Hole. There are also writing instruments, paper flowers, rubber stamps, paper crafts and Schminke watercolours. **Paperworks, 63 High Street ☎ 01803 867009.**

Textiles
Sally Carr has swept away any reminder of dry stuffy pastel cardie wool shops of yesteryear. Instead, there is a riotous assembly of gorgeous yarns, and a rail of irresistible handmade jackets, jumpers and cardigans. Everything for the adventurous and luxurious knitter, plus lots of inexpensive trinkets and toys for adults and children alike. **Sally Carr Designs, 31 High Street ☎ 01803 863060.**

Greenfibres
There's a powerful whiff of natural fibres from the reams of organic hemp, cotton, linen, and untreated silk on the shelves of Greenfibres' shop on the corner of Collins Road in The Narrows. The eco goods and garments sold here have been "produced in ways that do not harm the environment or exploit the people who

manufacture them", so there's every good reason to buy. Their mail order catalogue is exceedingly seductive for those who delight in the soft, pure and natural. How could babies wear anything other than the deliciously soft cotton underwear, completely untreated and undyed, and what about an organic linen shirt with coconut shell buttons? As for the duvets—organic cotton covered and filled with cashmere—heaven! **Greenfibres, 99 High Street ☎ 01803 868001.**

Stone Fabrics and Sewing Surgery Jane Starey got fed up with trekking up to London every time she needed fabric. Her daughters badgered her into doing something about it. She opened Stone Fabrics and Sewing Surgery in 1997. Specialising in natural silks and linens as well as high tech fabrics—fleece in particular—Stone Fabrics has a fabulous selection to choose from. Period buttons are a speciality, and don't miss Anthea Yeo's exquisite hand made buttons, or Vicky King's daisy silk ties. Jane also runs regular sewing surgeries for lapsed dressmakers and beginners. Classes are always for small numbers. Keep an eye out for occasional

Green Shoes workshop

Totnes

workshops—indigo dying, devouré, felt making, even hat making. Jane also offers a dressmaking service. **Stone Fabrics and Sewing Surgery, 97 High Street** ☎ 01803 868608.

Furniture

Tumblehome
Recycled and custom-built wooden furniture painted in Shaker colours, and a range of striking contemporary accessories are sold from this tiny showroom in Totnes High Street. Larger pieces are made to order. Discerning present-givers will be thankful to find that the choice of articles under a tenner have equally high standards of design. **Tumblehome Furniture, 5A High Street** ☎ 01803 863024 (shop) ☎ 01803 867032 (workshop).

Books

The Totnes Bookshop, owned by Dartington Hall Trust, is the main general bookshop in town. The friendly staff are ready with suggestions, whether it's for auntie's birthday or a local guidebook. **The Totnes Bookshop, 42 High Street** ☎ 01803 863273.

If you've a nose for a second-hand book, Totnes has a good selection. They fill the extensive shelves of **Pedlar's Pack** on The Plains—particularly good for Natural History, local interest and gardening. Half way up the hill is **The Bookshop**, for general interest out-of-print books, Opposite the Civic Square is **Harlequin**, with second-hand and remaindered books. Finally, at the top of town, is the enduring **Collards** in Castle Street. **Pedlar's Pack Books, 4 The Plains** ☎ 01803 866423. **The Bookshop, 72 Fore Street** ☎ 01803 864088. **Harlequin, 41 HighStreet** ☎ 01803 866406. **B. Collard Secondhand Books, 4 Castle Street** ☎ 01548 550246.

Arcturus Books and Crystals For a selection of alternative and complementary health titles, Arcturus Bookshop cuts the mustard. Subjects range from astrology through bodywork and personal growth to UFOs and ancient civilisations. There's also an absorbing noticeboard crammed with the offbeat. Coffee-table reading includes periodicals such as the *Ley Hunter Journal*, *Shamanism Channelled* and *Earth Mysteries*. **Arcturus, 47 Fore Street** ☎ 01803 864363.

Body and Soul

Hot Pursuit Bikes
Cycling locally, on Dartmoor for instance, requires a serious bicycle. Hot Pursuit is a serious shop with state-of-the-art machines and gear to go with them. Bicycles may be hired from here too. **Hot Pursuit, 44 Fore Street** ☎ 01803 865174.

Recycle The budget end of the bike market is catered for by Recycle, where bikes are available for hire and second-hand bikes are on sale. **Recycle, Civic Hall Shops, Market Square.**

The Float Centre Upstairs above Arcturus Bookshop is the calming Float Centre. A treatment here can, it is claimed, increase learning potential, improve sports performance, and alleviate aches and pains. 100 lbs of epsom salts is dissolved into 10 gallons of water warmed to body temperature, and the body is entirely supported by water. **The Float Centre, 47 Fore Street** ☎ 01803 864363.

In the same building is **the Centre for Oriental Medicine**, where nine practitioners offer consultations in herbal medicine, shiatsu, psychotherapy, acupressure and

Totnes

homeopathy. **Centre For Oriental Medicine, 47 Fore Street** ☎ 01803 868282.

Totnes Pavilion Besides a 25-metre, 4-lane swimming pool, a ten-seater sauna, gym, tennis courts, football and rugby pitches, the Pavilion also offers all kinds of activities throughout the year. Best to drop in to find out what's going on. **Totnes Pavilion, Borough Park** ☎ 01803 862992.

The Hair Sanctuary Tucked away in Bridgetown is this sanctuary from chemical treatments, cloying perfumes and general mistreatment of hair. The Hair Sanctuary uses organic products wherever possible, and they are highly skilled hair cutters, too. **The Hair Sanctuary, Post Cottage, Bridgetown** ☎ 01803 862505.

Roma Great haircuts downstairs, deliriously relaxing facials, massages etc upstairs. Roma uses the organic Aveda range of products, so no ethical pangs here. **Roma Hairdressing, 37 High Street** ☎ 01803 865724.

Bodyline Want to occupy those teenage girls for a while? Point them towards Bodyline, where

Roma Hairdressing

there is a wall lined with sparkly bits for nails, cheeks, hair and eyes. Upstairs in The Beauty Room there are seaweed facials for that special pamper; or, for as little as £4, the body may be decorated with a Mehndi henna tattoo (it fades after four weeks). **Bodyline, 24 Fore Street** ☎ 01803 863265.

Natural Health Centre Established back in 1978, the Totnes Natural Health Centre was the first of its kind in the UK. A wealth of different therapists and practitioners work from the centre. Some give treatments for donation; private sessions may be arranged. For relaxing treatments try aromatherapy, reiki, shiatsu or reflexology. **Natural Health Centre, Waterside, The Plains** ☎ 01803 864587.

Food Shops
Ticklemore Cheese Shop This small dairy has an excellent range of local cheeses as well as other British and European ones. Try the Beenleigh Blue, or Sharpham Brie. For the sweet-toothed, there is **Rocombe Dairy** ice cream in many of its delicious flavours. Ticklemore Cheese is a deservedly prize-winning business, supplying some of the best hotels, pubs

and restaurants. **Ticklemore Cheese Shop, 1 Ticklemore Street** ☎ 01803 865926.

Ticklemore Fish If you're stuck for a way to cook that pound of hake or halibut, turn to the folder of customers' seafood recipes, thoughtfully provided by Trudy Hunt of Ticklemore Fish. Daughter of a Brixham fisherman and a trained cook, Trudy knows her fish, which she snappily displays around a sawn-in-half dinghy. A tip: the splendid Kingfisher Fish and Chip Café will fry your Ticklemore skate wings for you. It's a bit of walk up the High Street, but worth it. **Ticklemore Fish, 10 Ticklemore Street, The Plains** ☎ 01803 867805. **Kingfisher Fish and Chips, 105 High Street** ☎ 867786.

Annie's Fruit and Veg Opposite Ticklemore Cheese is Annie's Fruit and Veg. This popular

Totnes

greengrocer sells extremely fresh vegetables and local eggs. The service is fast and helpful, and there's usually some local gossip to be picked up in the queue. **Annie's Fruit and Veg, Unit 4, Totnes Shopping Centre ☎ 01803 867265.**

Sacks Wholefoods Totnes wouldn't be Totnes without Sacks, with its familiar wholefoodie smell and unchanging layout. The mainstay of many a Totnesian, it holds a wide-ranging stock of anything the macrobiotic, vegan or vegetarian might require. Makes a change from Safeways. Prices are good, as is the produce. There is a small (but good) range of organic vegetables, as well as a compelling noticeboard. **Sacks Wholefoods, 80 High Street ☎ 01803 863263.**

A.W. Luscombe, Butcher A long-established family business, where meat is unceremoniously hauled down from its hook and

cut from the carcass. Luscombes have skilled and helpful butchers who will prepare cuts for you. Suppliers to the best local restaurants, the quality of this meat is exceptional. Be warned: if you ask for a joint for four, you might get rather more than you'd bargained for, as delicate portions aren't the stuff of Luscombes. Game can be ordered. **A.W. Luscombe, 48 Fore Street ☎ 01803 862119.**

Totnes Health Shop Seeds Bakery at Totnes Health Shop sells the most delicious wholemeal and sunflower loaves of bread. Fresh filled rolls and pies, moist cakes and slices fill their window—it's an ideal place to pick up a picnic. Try the very sustaining and utterly reliable egg mayonnaise and cress roll. **Totnes Health Shop, 35 High Street ☎ 01803 862526.**

Cranch's To pacify small people and give comfort to some big ones Cranch's sweet shop still sells sweets in jars: penny chews, fried eggs, gobstoppers, sherbert dips, and for the sophisticated customer chocolates hand-made in Chillington. **Cranch's, 35 Fore Street ☎ 01803 864437.**

Effings If you're an olive lover, wait until there's a good long queue to allow maximum tasting time for a wonderful range of olives. This small delicatessen stocks an extravagance of charcuterie, cheeses and patisseries. You can find poussin, soupe de poisson, guinea fowl, lemon tart and salmon en croute. There is a tiny café inside for continental-style cake-taking or rather special lunches. No ordinary place, no ordinary prices. **Effings, 50 Fore Street ☎ 01803 863435.**

Food For Thought Dipping out of shopping? Pick up a picnic at Food for Thought. Situated by the old marsh gates on the plains, Food for Thought stocks inventively filled pasties, olive bread, walnut bread, and a great range of tray bakes, all of which (and more) combined to win them a BBC Good Food award. A short walk away is Vire Island, and perfect for idle picnicking whilst watching the comings and goings on the river. **Food For Thought, 10 the Plains ☎ 01803 862071.**

Markets There are markets on Tuesdays, Fridays and Saturdays in Totnes. Visitors flock to the

Michael White of Sacks

Totnes

Tuesday morning Elizabethan market. On Friday and Saturday mornings there's a market in the Civic Square, which is a more local event. Arrive early (8ish) for the best pickings. Lots of second-hand stalls including china, antiques, clothes and tools. Fresh produce and plants are plentiful. A buzzy event, and a true focal point for locals.

Eating Out

Willow Wholefood Vegetarian Restaurant is run by a group of committed pure foodies. Their menu has an excellent selection of imaginative dishes, and there's always unfailingly good soup and bread to fall back on. In the back room there's a thoughtful children's corner, and a rack of ecologically sound mags. Outside in the leafy courtyard there's alfresco dining. Special Willow nights with themed food and music are held regularly. **Willow Wholefood Vegetarian Restaurant, 87 High Street ☎ 01803 862605.**

Café Sobrami On a summer morning, it's a lovely place for breakfast on the sunny terrace which overlooks the rooftops. Airy, continental-style café which serves fine coffee and cakes as well as a good line in all kinds of mediterranean cooking. **Café Sobrami, 82 High Street ☎ 01803 865522.**

Rumour Wine Bar More for the thirty-to-forty somethings. A classic wine bar formula, with occasional live music and faithful local support. Besides the *à la carte* menu there are generous bar snacks and wonderful home-made pizzas (with loads of runny toppings) which can be taken out. **Rumour Wine Bar, 30 High Street ☎ 01803 864682**

Greys Dining Room Immerse yourself in the warming ritual of afternoon tea at Greys, with its profusion of painted china and traditional metal teacake warmers. Home-made cakes, a selection of teas and fresh scones all come served in these reassuringly cosseted surroundings. **Greys Dining Rooms, 96 High Street ☎ 01803 866869.**

The Barrel House A dark continental atmosphere, often noisy and stuffed full of a changing array of junk. This is the place to catch up on gossip and 'hang out'. At night, convivial diners can be seen from the street, through the huge high

window of what was once a town ballroom. Try the garlic mushrooms and mozzarella on toast—or the fresh banana milkshake. **The Barrel House, 59a High Street ☎ 01803 863000.**

Rickshaws Nasi Goreng, seafood laksa, and coconut chicken are some of the South East Asian dishes authentically cooked at Rickshaws in the Narrows at the top of the High Street. If you fancy a taste of the exotic and a night in, you can also collect a take-away here. Why not pick up a Japanese, Russian, Czech or Mexican film from World Video, a few doors down the road? **Rickshaws, 95 High Street ☎ 01803 866171. World Video, 91 High Street ☎ 01803 866828.**

The Community Café Eating with toddlers can be tricky, and some cafés don't make it any easier. The Community Café takes it all in its stride,

Willow Vegetarian Restaurant

Totnes

serving homely food at good prices. Housed in what was the old grammar school, it forms part of a busy community centre running dozens of courses and activities. On the ground floor is an exhibition space which shows the work of local artists. **The Community Café, The Mansion, Fore Street ☎ 01803 862566.**

Places To Visit
Totnes Museum This small museum is worth visiting for its architecture alone. It is housed in a splendid Elizabethan building, built for local merchant William Kelland in 1575 (the layout of the original house still remains). Outside is the Tudor herb garden, authentically planted. The small scale of the museum is perfect for children, for whom there are special hands-on exhibits. Upstairs in the back room is the 'Nursery', filled with victorian toys and games. The Babbage Room commemorates Charles Babbage, inventor of the 'Difference Engine'—the first computer. **Totnes Museum, 70 Fore Street ☎ 01803 863821.**

The Guildhall Still used by the Totnes Town Council, the panelled hall with wooden 'throne' seats has seen the inauguration of an awful lot of mayors since 1359. Children will thrill to see the old town cells, peep at the old mayoral robes or hear the tale of the ghost on the stairway. At the time of writing, the curator is Bob Mann, author of *The Ghosts of Totnes*. He has many a shivering tale to tell of the town. **The Guildhall, Ramparts Walk ☎ 01803 862147.**

Trips from Totnes

Here are two outings from Totnes. The first takes a trip down Longmarsh beside the river. The second follows the riverside walk to Dartington, joining the cycle path which links to the Cider Press Craft Centre.

1. A Short Stroll to Longmarsh

For a riverside stroll which is also bike-able, buggyable and wheelchair friendly, try Longmarsh. Cross Charles Fowler's bridge into Bridgetown (that's what they call the settlement over the water) and take the first road on the right. First right again and you will be heading along Steamer Quay, beside the Dart. Little ones always enjoy spending ages on the wooden play galleon beside the Riverside Café—but don't let them linger too long;

Beside the Dart at Lon

follow the road to the car park, then the path between the river and new marine-inspired industrial units, until you reach the Rowing Club. On early mornings or winter Sunday afternoons you'll be made to feel an instant couch potato upon seeing the teams of rowers sculling over the surface of the water in pond-skater fashion. The green space beyond the next car park offers an accessible riverside path, with hand-carved seating providing welcome stops. Longmarsh was once used by the local rifle volunteers, and you can still find the remains of the rifle butts at the far side of the strip of unusually (for South Devon) flat land.

The open space—once all saltmarsh—is a favourite with local families and dog walkers, and can be busy on Sunday afternoons. It is still a good space to admire the river as it flows away from the town, to walk in tall grass and be surrounded by clouds of butterflies in summer, and to pick blackberries in autumn.

2. A Walk around the Dartington Estate

In the 1920s, the American heiress Dorothy Whitney-Straight and her English husband, the agriculturalist Leonard Elmhirst, established a 'centre for experiments in rural reconstruction and progressive education' on a dilapidated estate bordering the river Dart at Dartington. Influenced by the progressive social ideas of Indian poet and thinker Rabindranath Tagore, and heeding his advice that they look for somewhere in Devon because of the softness of the landscape and gentleness of climate, they bought the 800-acre mediæval estate, complete with deer park, home farm and Great Hall. Over the next forty years they developed a diverse community of artists, educationalists and agriculturalists with two schools, innovative forestry and agricultural methods, a pottery, a famous glassworks, a textile mill, a centre for the arts and an international summer school of music. Today, although much has changed, the vision and philosophy of the original founders remain intact, and continues to inform the many and diverse projects undertaken at Dartington. As a forestry man, Leonard Elmhirst was inclined to 'follow the way the sap was flowing'. Now the sap flows in many different directions on the estate. This can make the place rather hard to navigate, especially for a visitor; there's always more to find out. It's part of the draw of the place, as has been the case for the past seventy-five years.

For walking around the estate, the most popular path follows the river. This may be picked up just beyond where the cycle path hangs a left beside Berryman's Marsh. On the right, shortly after the second gate posts (where the road narrows), are a gate and stile which lead into a field beside the river. This path follows a riverside route through North Wood to Huxham's Cross, where it is possible to pick up the public footpath, which returns to the drive just beyond Dartington Lodge, via the Cider Press and the cycle path.

A Riverside Walk

From Totnes it is possible to take a riverside walk and cycle path to the Dartington estate. The path starts at the Old Bridge in Totnes on the town side of the river, and eventually emerges on to the Dartington estate drive just below the lodge entrance. This is also a wheelchair and buggy-friendly path (radar keys for the gates along the path can be hired from the Tourist Information Centre in the Town Mill, Totnes, just beside the pedestrian exit from Safeway's car park). Either side of the drive at this point are water meadows. These were once an arm of the river Dart, with boats carrying their cargo as far up as The Queen's Arms pub. Berryman's Marsh, on the river side of the drive, was set aside in 1991 to create a wetland habitat (attracting rare species of birds), wildflowers and grasses. It follows a route beside the water meadow along the edge of the woodland to Shinner's Bridge, emerging at a cluster of workshops and shops around the **Cider Press Centre.**

After passing the old Tweed Mills and the two lime kilns for the estate, you will find **Dartington Pottery** on the right. Founded by Bernard Leach in the 1920s, it was here that he wrote *A Potter's Book*. Leach's involvement in Dartington lasted only five years, but his influence lives on, and the craft of pottery thrives. This is also due in part to the availability of good clay, for both ball and china clay are found in Devon.

Dart Pottery—as it is now known—produces the joyful and flamboyant designs of Janice Tchalenko. A hallmark of her work is that the designs cover all surfaces of the pot. Apple, Peacock, Orchid and Delphinium are the names of some of her bold designs, which are applied using sponges, brushes or slip trailers, giving a sense of immediacy and lightness of touch. Seconds are on sale at the Pottery shop for substantially less than the cost of a 'first'.

Further along the path is **Tridias**, which you enter at your peril, for this spacious, browsable toy shop holds a captivating range of toys and games, as well as an excellent book and tape section. The emphasis is on invention, from the potato clock to the spangly fairy outfit. The extensive 'hands on' Brio table serves to distract the children, allowing furtive

FROM STONE TO PAINT

The large stone 'fireplaces' beside the Dartington Pottery are a pair of disused lime kilns. These can often be found dotted around the banks of the Dart, for the limestone and coal which they burnt together to produce lime was easier to transport by barge than by packhorse through Devon's muddy lanes. The business part of the kilns are behind the grates.

Here there is an inverted 'bottle' which was filled from the top. The steep path to the right of the kilns allowed a horse and cart to reach the top and tip in layers of limestone, coal and timber. The slow burning caused a chemical reaction, which resulted in a white lime dust which could be shovelled out from the grate.

In this area of damp and often acid hills, lime was a vital commodity which improved the fertility of the the predominantly acid soil. Mixed with water and sand, it also made a cement for building walls, and mixed to a 'milk' with water it made a limewash paint.

purchases to be made. If you haven't the time to pause, pick up a catalogue and buy by mail order. **Tridias, Cider Press Centre, Dartington ☎ 01803 863957.**

Walking towards the main entrance of the Cider Press, you will find the **Book Shop**. It is worth dropping in here, if only for the idiosyncratic nature of the stock, which reflects both the community it comes from and the image it projects. Big on philosophy, poetry and all kinds of making, with lots of handsome books to browse through. **The Book Shop ☎ 01803 864171.**

Mind out for wandering jugglers as you cross the courtyard into the main Cider Press, which I shall deal with briefly as it is so well covered in mainstream guides, save to note one exhibit in the craft shop: the pottery of **Marianne De Trey**. Back in 1949 she took over the pottery at Dartington, and ran it for many years. Her pots are delicately understated, in porcelain and celadin. Now well into her eighties, De Trey is still working at Shinner's Bridge in the workshop built for David Leach all those years ago. **The Cider Press Centre, Dartington ☎ 01803 864171.**

Back on to the cycle path, which is picked up beyond the plant shop and additional car parks. Follow the footpath past Dartington cricket pitch to the left, and Foxhole to the right; this building once housed the famous progressive Dartington School, where pupils involved themselves in the small rural businesses of Dartington as part of their self-guided educational programme. William Curry, the first headmaster

of the School and a passionate believer in modernism, was instrumental in employing the Swiss American architect William Lescaze to design **High Cross House**—the headmaster's house—a little further up the drive. Distinguished by brave blue walls and sharp geometric lines, it contrasts starkly with the soft grey stone of nearby buildings. Carefully restored over recent years, and furnished with pieces of its time and place, this 1932 international modernist house makes for an inspiring visit. Inside, amongst the rounded edges of the 1930s decor and furniture, are paintings and ceramics from the private collection which Dorothy and Leonard Elmhirst bequeathed to the Dartington Hall Estate. Concentrating upon the early part of the twentieth century, it comprises paintings (including Cecil Collins and Ben Nicholson), ceramics (including Leach and Hamada), and private press books, typography and illustration (including Eric Gill). The Dartington Archive is also held here, made up of letters, books, photographs, films and tapes accumulated since 1925 (viewing by appointment only). Further examples of International Modernist style buildings to be found on the estate include those in Warren Lane, a particularly fine example being Warren House, which was built complete with dance floor, serpentine wall and sun-bathing balconies for the dancer Kurt Joos, who was resident there during the 1930s. **High Cross House, Dartington ☎ 01803 864114.** Open from May to the end October. Entrance £2.50 (£1.50 concessions). It is also possible to hire the rooms for special occasions.

Between High Cross House and Foxhole is the **Regional Centre for Organic Horticulture,**

LUCCOMBE'S COFFIN

The original Luccombe oak was propagated in 1763 from a hybrid seedling which retained its leaves throughout the winter. At the age of around 70, William Luccombe had the tree cut down, and planks from it were stored under his bed. Thirty years later, when he eventually died at the age of 102, it was used to make his coffin.

Dartington. Primarily a horticultural training centre, the organic produce grown here supplies the Dartington kitchens and local shops; any surplus is sold to the public. This can include vegetables, herbs, cut flowers, and all kinds of salads. Availability depends upon the season—it's a case of pot luck. As I write, plans are afoot to open a shop. **Regional Centre for Organic Horticulture** ☎ 01803 867693. Open 9.30–4.00 weekdays.

At Huxham's Cross, close to the church, can be found SPARC (South Devon Play and Resource Centre) scrap store, which sells materials and equipment for making every imaginable thing. Somewhere amongst rolls of coloured plastic sacks, fleece offcuts, reams of ribbon, and sundry discards from local industry, can be found co-ordinators Ali Roscoe and Caroline Lakin. Join the scrap store and you can fill a bag with chosen pieces for £1, as well as purchase good quality art materials at very low cost. Workshops for making jewellery, costumes and seasonal decorations are held for children (and adults) in Dartington and outlying villages. There's also a ball pool, badge-making machine and parachute for hire from here, and if you're stuck for ideas a craftbook library. In the summer months they offer a week's membership, which is a godsend if it rains for a day or two of your holiday. To reach the Scrapstore, make for the public car parks at Shinner's Bridge; just to the left of the entrances to these, pick up the cycle path which runs between a field and a hedge. The path emerges opposite The Old Postern (which houses Schumacher College); walk down to Dartington Church, turn right along the main road for a short distance, then pick up the footpath signed to Huxhams Cross. Make for the covered yard full of boxes of scrap beyond the wooden-fronted building. **SPARC, Huxham's Cross, Dartington. For opening hours** ☎ 01803 868036.

TURKEY OAK

Between the College buildings at Lower Close and the entrance to the White Hart is a majestic turkey oak. Under the shade of this tree are planted hundreds of croci, which when in flower form a vast purple disc. Pilgrimages are made to see them and to say goodbye to winter.

The Courtyard

ROBINS AT DARTINGTON

Dartington Hall grounds are filled with birdlife and beautiful flowers. Ian Mercer, who was for many years chief officer of Dartmoor National Park, used to lead an annual common bird census in the grounds. The most common bird at Dartington is the robin, and it was here that some of the secrets of the robin's life were first discovered.

There was a young teacher, David Lack, teaching at Dartington Hall School. In 1934 he began a study of the robins living in the grounds. During four years he ringed 119 adults and 121 nestlings. To study their habits at close quarters he constructed two aviaries, both ten yards long, where the robins bred successfully. When the young were fledged, David Lack let them and their parents free.

In the autumn he found that about three-quarters of the females disappeared and did not return until the early spring. The males and the remaining quarter of the females stayed, having individual winter territories.

He listened to the song of the robin, and found that the spring song started in late December and continued until mid-June. He first heard the thinner, autumn song in late July, and this continued—a sad, weak reflection of the vigorous song of spring—until the spring song started again in December. In the autumn he discovered that not only the males sang: about half of the female robins were also singing.

Robins can live for about ten years, but David Lack revealed from ringing recoveries that average life expectancy is only just over a year. He pointed out that if there were no sparrowhawks, weasels, cats or disease, in ten years one pair would have multiplied to two million.

Robins use their red breasts for display, reinforcing the message of their song that this patch is theirs and intruders should go away. David Lack bought a tatty stuffed robin and placed it by some of the robins' nests, when they had young. The parents attacked it violently, in one case beheading the lifeless creature. He decided to develop the experiment, removing all of the parts of the bird until only a tuft of red breast feathers were left. Most of the robins still attacked the specimen. In contrast, when he painted over the breast of another stuffed robin with brown paint the Dartington robins took no notice.

Around Dartington Hall

Just up the hill from the entrance to the Courtyard is **The Gallery**, with a small exhibition space and the offices of **Dartington Arts**. Here information can be gathered about what's on, and bookings made for a wide range of concerts, films (a regular programme at **The Barn** theatre), and performances. Although a small place, Dartington has an international reputation for both mainstream and  experimental arts, and attracts artists of a very high calibre. Watch out too for free events, especially during the International Summer School season (July–August), which is awash with concerts and recitals. The degree shows at the College of Arts (in June) indicate the directions of contemporary arts and new media. **Dartington Arts Box Office ☎ 01803 863073.**

Not free, but particularly good value, are the plays put on by the Dartington Playgoers. Each summer this amateur dramatic society—with more than a peppering of ex-professionals amongst them—puts on Shakespeare in the gardens. There are at least one or two other Playgoers' productions per season, and these (more than the weather) are reliably good. Make a summer's evening of it: walk up to Dartington, and take a light supper at **The White Hart**—the restaurant and pub in the courtyard, to the left of the entrance to the Great Hall. This can be followed by a walk in the gardens before catching a film or a show. And if the walk back seems all too much, call a taxi.

Dartington Hall Gardens Below The Gallery and to the right is the arched entrance to the courtyard—with the newly renovated Barn Theatre on the left inside the archway. Take the path across the courtyard and past The White Hart into the gardens.

Dorothy Elmhirst absorbed herself in the making of this 'English Garden' for over 40 years, involving amongst others the American landscape gardener Beatrix Farrand. Trees in the gardens are particularly remark-

DARTINGTON YOUTH HOSTEL

If the acronym YHA fills you with visions of toil lists, emptying latrines and single sex dorms with lights out by 9.30, then take a look at the Dartington Youth Hostel. This sixteenth-century cottage and annexe stands beside Bidwell Brook in an idyllic hamlet close to Dartington. It makes an ideal base from which to explore the locality. Inexpensive accommodation is in five- or six-bedded rooms, and family rooms can be booked if available. In winter, when the hostel is closed, it is possible to book the whole place—ideal for those extended family 'do's', or for getting together with a bunch of friends on neutral territory. **Dartington Youth Hostel, Lownyard, Dartington, Totnes, Devon TQ9 6JJ ☎ 01803 862303.**

able, with many of the finest dating from the nineteenth century, and Spanish chestnuts above the terraces are thought to be from the mid-sixteenth century. Luccombe oaks, of which there are two, are thought to be from the original planting by the Exeter nurseryman William Luccombe.

Numerous paths have been carved through the gardens, moving from formal to informal planting. Each season brings something special. In winter the skeleton of the garden is exposed, and vistas are cleared. In spring, the magnolias and camellias come into their own (the Camellia Walk was one of Beatrice Ferrand's introductions to the garden). In summer, the demonstrative herbaceous border mixes soft yellows, mauves and blues in a pattern which repeats itself every second wall column. In Autumn the foliage is a riot of pinks, yellows, oranges and reds. Children love the space of the gardens—one of the thatched huts now used by the gardeners was built as a Wendy house for the young Elmhirst children. Kids have a ball leaping up and down flights of steps, making entrances from behind the clipped hedge wings of the open air theatre in the Tilt-yard, and discovering dens and secret pathways. Sadly, the temptation to roly-poly down the terraces above the Tiltyard must be resisted. The Dartington Hall Gardens are open daily. Suggested donation £2.00. A *Guide to the Gardens* (by Reginald Snell) is available at Reception, under the arch in the entrance to the courtyard.

Annual events to note

Ways with Words A literary fortnight in early summer (usually July) with a surfeit of workshops, talks, readings, and lunches, drawing the literati together at Dartington. Kay Dunbar, the local organiser of this festival, brings together both crowd-pulling names and more marginal, off-beat speakers. Take the opportunity to catch some bright stars of the literary skies. **Ways With Words, Droridge Farm ☎ 01803 867311.**

Riverford Farm Pumpkin Day One day a year, towards the end of October, Riverford Organic Vegetables have a Pumpkin Day at Wash Farm, Staverton. Pumpkins mark the route so you don't get lost in the lanes. Visitors get a bumpy trailer ride around the farm, a talk about how it all works, and a chance to collect vegetables from the fields (don't forget to bring a bag). Then it's back to a shed heaving with pumpkins, and piping hot soup. A great family outing. Proceeds go to Oxfam. **Riverford Organic Vegetables, Wash Barn, Buckfastleigh ☎ 01803 762720.**

The Raft Race A chilly autumn diversion on the first Sunday in October, which sends rafts and their makers hurtling down a frisky River Dart from Buckfastleigh to Staverton. People come from all over the country to participate. Stand by Totnes Weir and watch them struggle to keep their rafts in one piece!

Sculpture by Henry Moore in Dartington Hall gardens

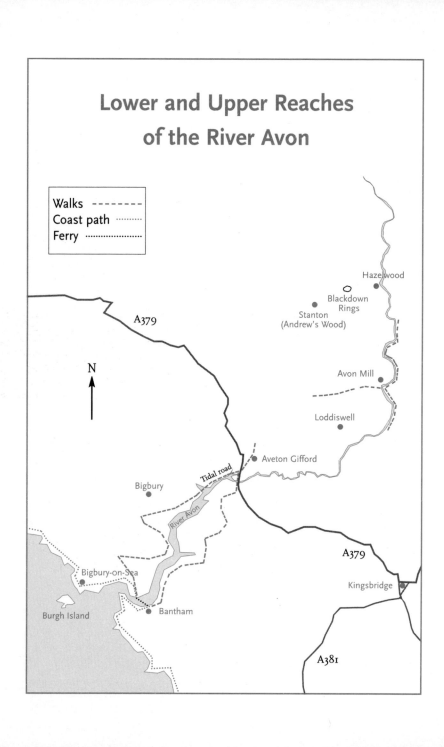

Lower and Upper Reaches
of the River Avon

Walks   --------
Coast path   ··········
Ferry   ···················

Hazelwood

Blackdown
Rings
Stanton
(Andrew's Wood)

A379

N

Avon Mill

Loddiswell

Aveton Gifford

Tidal road

Bigbury

River Avon

A379

Bigbury-on-Sea

Kingsbridge

Burgh Island

Bantham

A381

Chapter 4—Avon Valley

Beginning in Bantham, this chapter covers two separate stretches of the River Avon. The first is a walk around the stretch of tidal estuary, from the ferry crossing point at Bantham, up to Aveton Gifford and back along the east bank of the estuary to Bantham. The second stretch starts with Blackdown Rings and Andrew's Wood (Stanton Moor), then moves to the Hazelwood Estate, the village of Loddiswell, and a walk in the higher Avon Valley.

The River Avon keeps a low profile, as South Devon rivers go. It remains relatively unspoilt and undeveloped, for sandy banks at the river mouth prevent its use by all but small craft. Because of this, the Avon Estuary has resisted the 'boaty' image of its neighbours, the Kingsbridge and Salcombe Estuary and the Dart. Instead it offers long stretches of peaceful riverside walks, through exceptional countryside packed with wildlife.

Firstly it is the area south of Loddiswell that we explore—the Lower Reaches—with its broad valley, which progresses gently through marshland, on through woodland and several dispersed farmsteads, to the sea.

The Lower Reaches

Bantham Bantham has a wide expanse of sandy bay where the waves break far enough out to make it one of the few surfing beaches around. Kite enthusiasts meet here regularly to take advantage of the strong

Bantham beach

PLANTS AROUND BANTHAM

The grass that flourishes in the sand dunes at Bantham is a remarkable plant. It is called marram grass, and only really thrives in moving sand. It brings about its own destruction, for the vast underground network of roots it pushes out through moving sand consolidate it, so that it no longer moves. As the tall tussocks above ground grow, they provide a place where other plants may become established. The arching leaves of the marram are grooved so that they can curve round in the heat of the day, closing up like a drainpipe, keeping moisture from evaporating. I love watching, early in the morning, drops of dew dripping off the tips of the marram grass leaves and making tiny crater like depressions in the sand.

Inland from the sand dunes, where the marram is dying and other grasses are taking over, you can find large patches of iris. This is stinking iris, which is most at home on chalky soil. In summer, it has beautifully veined purple flowers; they look wonderful but smell horrid. In Autumn, the big seed-pods open to reveal lots of orange berries, which to someone's eyes must have resembled underdone meat for another name for it is 'roast beef plant'.

If you search diligently you may find the pale pink pyramids of the pyramidal orchid. In June and early July it grows among the fine grasses. I first found it growing on the chalk downs of Kent, but it is equally at home at Bantham and Bigbury.

Bantham is also a paradise for butterflies. Look out for the black and white marbled whites, the blues, the browns, and the migrant painted ladies. Also the six-spot burnet, a day-flying moth which lays its eggs on the 'eggs and bacon' flowers of bird's-foot-trefoil. Look out for the green and black chequered caterpillars nibbling the leaves or climbing a stem to make its cocoon, like a vertical golden hammock. The moths zoom about on sunny days. It is only when they are still resting upon yellow ragwort blossom or purple knapweed, sipping nectar through their long black tongues, that their black wings, seared with scarlet lines and spots, are visible.

winds which can batter this part of the
coast. On gentler days, it can be perfect for
a trip to the beach with the kids, the sand
being ideal for castles, and the sea for
swimming where it is designated safe. The
beach is reached by a single track road
which passes through the pretty village of
Bantham. Sadly this is all too often
obscured by a scrum of traffic on a
summer's day. It has, amongst other
things, a good pub, **The Sloop Inn**, which
sells real ales and local cider, and whose restaurant specialises in seafood
dishes. **The Sloop Inn, Bantham ☎ 01548 560215.**

'Ham' being Saxon for settlement, it is probable that Bantham Ham
was an ancient settlement. Certainly excavations suggest that it was once
an iron age settlement and trading centre. Archæological finds hereabouts, such as fish hooks, pottery, bone tools and javelin heads, have
been dated from between Iron Age and mediæval periods. In the second
half of the ninth century the Danes raided Devon, but failed to establish
a foothold in Bigbury Bay. A bloody battle was fought and won at
Bantham Ham on the eve of Epiphany, in which many Danes were

THE HUMBLE PILCHARD

A large scale pilchard fishery operated
around Bigbury Bay, Salcombe and
Hope Cove for hundreds of years.
Cellars still exist where the fish were
stored and cured. Close to the Pilchard
Inn on Burgh Island, which lies directly
out to sea from Bantham Ham, was a
'huers' hut, where a lookout was posted
to spot the shimmer of a shoal of
pilchard. The fish could number in the
millions, discolouring the water as far
back as the horizon. At the cry, fleets of
small boats would pour out of the Avon
to enclose the fish in colossal nets, or
they were literally scooped up by hand

from the water. They were preserved in
hogsheads or stone pallaces with salt
from the local saltern; or air dried,
packed in barrels and shipped to
Europe to Catholic countries. Pilchard
oil was used to light the lamps of
Bantham. Dotted around the coast are
pilchard cellars, houses and stations.
Not surprisingly, the pilchard was over-
fished, and had all but disappeared
from this coastline by the late 1800s.

'Craim on pilchards' is a local saying,
meaning clean on the outside but dirty
within.

The Sloop Inn at Bantham

slaughtered. For centuries after, the eve of Epiphany was celebrated to mark this victory. The fact that ancient human remains have been found in some quantities around the Ham in recent years, adds some substance to the story.

Sticks It is worth noting, particularly if a long walk is about to be taken, that the stick-maker Henry Alexander lives in the village. He first learned the technique as a boy scout, and 47 years on he makes superlative walking sticks from a variety of local woods—ash, blackthorn, sweet chestnut, burr elm, honeysuckle, twisted alder and oak. Wonderful objects, and functional to boot—essential equipment for walking the hills of South Devon. Visit by appointment ☎ **01548 561182.**

A Walk along the Avon Estuary

This nine-mile waymarked walk starts at Bantham, crosses the Avon to Bigbury, follows a path along the west side of the river to Aveton Gifford, and returns on the opposite bank to Bantham. It would be useful to pick up a copy of the Avon Valley walk leaflet or Aveton Gifford's guided walk and village trail maps before setting out. Beginning from Bantham, it is possible to cross the river by the foot ferry from May 25–September 5 (not Sundays) between 10am–11am and 3pm–4pm. Other times can be arranged at the discretion of the ferryman. To get to the foot ferry, turn right before the entrance to the car park and follow the path down to the water. The departure point is beside the thatched waterside home—inside which beautiful clinker-built open boats are constructed. The ferry is one of these, adding a particular pleasure to this short trip. **Foot ferry information ☎ 01548 561196 and ask for ferryman Neil Schroeter.**

Once across the water, follow the 'Heron' signs. A steep climb crosses Bigbury golf course, and leads into open fields. By now the views are opening up. The route moves between the fields and woods of the Evans Estate. At the widest part of the estuary—Stiddicombe Creek—the sand and mud flats attract all manner of birds. August and September see the arrival of the waders on autumn migration. These include curlew, oyster-catchers, lapwing, redshank, greenshank, ringed plover and dunlin. On occasions avocet, sanderling, knot and lesser yellow legs have been seen.

The east bank of the Avon at Bantham

The route eventually joins the tidal road which is impassable for about **two hours** either side of high tide. Turn left here if tempted by the lure of seafood, for Avon Oysters is about 200 yards up the road on the right hand side.

Avon Oysters This oyster farm grows plump pacific oysters—'Pacific Gigas'—with a wonderful salty taste and deep cupped shells. Samphire from the banks of the Avon is on sale here in July and August, as are locally caught crabs and lobsters, and locally smoked salmon, trout and mackerel. Crawfish may be ordered. Alongside Avon Oysters is the delightful **Oyster Shack** where tables and chairs are set out under a vine- and honeysuckle-shaded canopy. This 'unlicensed and seasonal' eating place is the stuff of gorgeous lazy lunches, where, because the food is so fresh and delicious, one wants to try everything. Bringing your own wine keeps the cost down. It's a busy place, so book well in advance to ensure a table. **Open Wednesday through Saturday 12.30–2.30 ☎ 01548 810876**.

The Oyster House at Bigbury-on-Sea opened in 1999. Run by the same family, it has the same relaxed and easy atmosphere as Avon Oysters, and serves a similar menu, only this café is licensed. Open

COB BUILDINGS IN BANTHAM

Many of the houses in Bantham are made from cob, a traditional Devon building material. This is straw and earth mixed together, then packed together on top of a stone base, in lifts of around two to three feet. These are then compacted by foot and trimmed back to form a neat face. The cob then dries, forming a strong wall. It was a lengthy process, costing very little, aside from labour. Cob buildings were made from earth dug close to the site, so the colour and texture of the cob varies according to the soil. Farm buildings were often left unrendered, thus matching the earth from which they were built. Houses made from cob have particular qualities: the thick breathable walls allow coolness in summer and warmth in winter. Curves are a characteristic of cob, the earth mixture being more malleable than brick or stone. Cob houses were traditionally finished with lime renders which were either left white, or tinted by natural earth pigments.

Boats at Bantham

Tuesday–Sunday 12.30–2.30, and evenings on
Friday and Saturday ☎ 01548 810676.

It's a good thing seafood is energising, for there
are a few more miles to cover yet. Go down the hill
to the Tidal Road, which leads eventually to Stakes
Road, where (as the name implies) a sequence of
stakes marks the way. Before the road was metalled
it was made up from a line of stepping stones,
known to locals as the 'dog biscuits', which marked
the route. Follow the path to Timbers car park in
Aveton Gifford. The parish map on display in the
car park provides a useful guide to the village and
its history.

Aveton Gifford

The early fifteenth-century long bridge at Aveton Gifford still takes the
load of traffic which used to thunder through the main street of the
village. Until recently, living in the heart of Aveton Gifford wasn't fun,
and the years of having to close their front doors to keep out the noise
and fumes caused the community to become fragmented. This was put
right when, in the mid-1980s, a bypass was finally completed; people got

THE BUSH CRICKET

After walking southwards down the length of the tidal
road, search among the saltmarsh vegetation
beyond the little car park: you may see coneheads
leaping from leaf to leaf on the tall green club
rushes. These are a type of bush cricket, a little
insect like a grasshopper but with over-long antennae
and orange eyes on stalks. Their green and black bodies are long
and slender, and the female has an ovipositor—a sword with which
to lay eggs—curving from her back end.

Figurehead on thatched house at Bantham

together and set about designing a parish map, a town trail and a guided walk. Today, Aveton Gifford is once more a thriving community, as it was in earlier days when the harmonium was heaved aboard the village barge, and the Methodist Church Sunday School set off down river singing their hearts out all the way to Bantham.

The Village Trail Stand pipes, staddle stones, hitching rings, a tyring platform, and Lady Arch are just some of the things to find on the Village Trail. Incidentally, number fourteen on the trail—the sixteenth century farmhouse at **Court Barton**, owned by the Balkwill family, serves scrumptious farmhouse teas. **Court Barton ☎ 01548 550312.**

The Village Trail and the **Riverside Walk leaflets** maps are available at Aveton Gifford Post Office. For flagging members of your party, ordering a taxi for the return trip to Bantham is an option at this point.

Back to Bantham To walk off the tea, cross Long Bridge to the east side of the river and follow the waymarked route, which continues through green lanes, around creeks and over fields, before returning to the broadening vistas of Bantham where the mouth of the Avon ends.

Avon Valley

The Upper Reaches
In this second section of the Avon, we explore an area north of Loddiswell where the river flows fast through the narrow steep-sided valley, through dense woodland and lush flora. There is no convenient network of public footpaths to link the areas covered here, partly because of issues of land ownership, but also because some areas are very sensitive as they support rare wildlife species. Because of the special nature of this area, we shall treat this section as a series of discrete places.

1.Blackdown Rings and Andrew's Wood

The Avon flows southward, past Topsham Bridge and through the steep wooded valleys now under the guardianship of the Woodland Trust. On the heights either side of the valley stand the iron age hill forts of Stanborough and Blackdown Rings.

On occasions, it's a relief to climb up to such heights, above the shadow and shelter of the hills, to get a larger sense of the South Hams. At six hundred and forty feet above sea level, **Blackdown Rings**, a couple of miles north of Loddiswell, is just such a place. At this exposed and ancient site, which is studded with wind-battered oaks and blackthorn, a helpful directional map identifies landmarks round 360 degrees, with Dartmoor to the north, Totnes to the north-east, Dartmouth to the east and Start Bay to the south-west. Blackdown Rings takes its name from the vast earthworks which encircle the hilltop, an Iron Age fort which was built around 400 BC. The earthworks are still visible, as are the motte and bailey castle constructed by the Normans after the conquest in 1066. Rabbits now burrow in the Iron Age embankment, and 'sausage lichens' blow in the wind from the gnarled oak trees growing in the Iron Age ditch. Blackdown was one of the last areas of the South Hams to become cultivated, remaining as heathland until quite recently. Lead was mined here for a short time in the nineteenth century, but the site has been left unexcavated. Once a part of the Hazelwood estate, it is now owned by the Arundell Charity, which was founded in 1591 by Sir Matthew Arundell 'for the good and behoof of parishioners of Loddiswell'. This landmark is a site to bring a kite to on a clear blue day and get blown all over the place. A leaflet about Blackdown Rings is available at the Tourist Information Centre in Kingsbridge.

Andrew's Wood isn't signed on the main road. The discreet car park is a turning to the left off the road beyond **MGM Nurseries** and before Blackdown Rings. There are two marked routes through this remarkable woodland, both well within the capacities of small children: the 'Frog' route is the shorter, and the 'Ant' route slightly longer. Both move between woods and clearings on well constructed walkways, bridges and stepping stones. The detailed guide book fleshes out the walks with fascinating information about some of the things which can be seen in the different

ANDREW'S WOOD

Only half a mile's walk away from Blackdown Rings is Andrew's Wood, or Stanton Moor as it used to be known. Stanton Moor was a group of fields—mostly rough pasture—with a small farm at the southern end. In the middle of the nineteenth century the farm fell into disuse, and some of the wet fields were invaded by seedlings from the mature trees on the hedgebanks. Birch and pussy willow came first, oak slowly followed, and after half a century it was shading out the short-lived birch. As the century progressed, more fields fell into disuse. It was here at Stanton Moor that Reverend Keble Martin and other botanists found the heath lobelia in the 1890s. It was a rare plant then, and now it only grows on six sites in Britain. In the 1960s Col. and Mrs Walker owned Stanton Moor, and the neighbouring farm and house of Woolston. Their son Andrew, who loved the woodland and old pasture fields, was killed in a road accident while serving in the army. Upon leaving the area shortly after his death, Andrew's parents sold Stanton Moor to the Devon Wildlife Trust, on condition that it should from now on be known as Andrew's Wood, in memory of their son.

The purple-blue spikes of the heath lobelia are to be seen at their best in bloom during July and August, growing up to 2 ft 6 inches high in clearings around the wood. Also found in the the clearings are the rare ragged-robin, heath spotted and marsh orchids, yellow bartsia, devil's-bit scabious and royal fern. The tufted grasses and rushes are equally important. Willow warblers and tree pipits, migrants from Africa, nest in tussocks. Adders and lizards bask on the warm quartzite boulders. In early Spring, the brimstone butterfly is one of the first to emerge. Then in midsummer the silver-washed fritillaries (our largest butterfly) emerge, their orange upper wings delicately lined with black, the underwings rippled with waves of silver. Resting on the woodland paths can be seen the speckled wood butterfly.

In winter, the tussocks that shelter birds nests in summer now provide extra insulation for the hibernating dormice in their winter nests. They are snugly rolled up inside thick balls of grass.

ADDENDUM

Fifty-one deaths were recorded in and around Loddiswell in 1590 between 16th March and 12th September. A number of the victims were registered as coming from and around Stanton Moor. Afterwards, locals regarded the moor as an unhealthy spot. One Loddiswell woman remembered being told when she was a girl in the late 1800s not to go there for fear of disease. It followed that the heath was let alone, it seems, for centuries. Perhaps this explains the extraordinary wealth of wildlife flora and fauna it supports.

seasons. Should you wish for a guided walk or even a 'nature watch' in Andrew's Wood, they are sometimes included in the calendars of events produced by Devon Wildlife Trust and the Coast and Countryside Service. A *Guide to Andrew's Wood* by Gordon Waterhouse is on sale at Loddiswell Village shop, or at the Tourist Information Centre in Kingsbridge.

2. Hazelwood Estate

It was the draw of the extraordinary Avon valley which brought a group of women together to purchase sixty-four acres of the Hazelwood Estate in 1989. They would shudder to be called a community; rather a bunch of individuals thrown together, who have invented this unique centre. The house itself takes guests and runs courses, alongside a programme of esoteric events. In addition there are four self-catering cottages on the steeply sloping valley which tumbles down to the River Avon. The co-owners of **Hazelwood House** are also involved with an international peace initiative called 'Peace through Understanding', and have hosted refugees from many parts of the world. Coincidentally the Quaker founder of the estate, Richard Peake, directed his energies and wealth from the tea trade towards the spread of peace principles. He financed the building of the churches in Loddiswell and Ugborough, as well as supporting less well-heeled Tory candidates.

The financing of the current Hazelwood project has been a struggle, and the upkeep of the elderly buildings quite a challenge. Opportunities exist for volunteers to work on the estate, planting, renovating, or scrub clearing. Contact Hazelwood House for more details. Gold, silver, and pure spring water (bottled at source—ideal for babies—and available at the house) have all been discovered around Hazelwood. An elderly pollarded oak stands beside the entrance to the house. Inside, the dimly lit hall,

Hazelwood boathouse

smelling of wood smoke, leads into a series of homely rooms, well worn and relaxed. Rooms are comfortably furnished in ad hoc style.

Hazelwood remains purposefully 'off-line' (mail outs are quaintly hand-written)—but for how much longer—who knows? There's certainly an off-season appeal. It would be the ideal place to retreat in midwinter, for books, walks and reflection—a great way to get away from the telly.

For a programme of events and details of accommodation, contact Hazelwood Estate, Loddiswell, Kingsbridge ☎ 01548 821232.

3. Loddiswell

Loddiswell village—or Lodda's well, three hundred feet above sea level, has one of the few village greens in the South Hams. In 1850 Loddiswell was listed as having three mills, four tailors, one woolcomber, cattle and pigs (providing leather for the bootmaker), a blacksmith, a wheelwright and three inns. A family called Luscombe manufactured yellow ochre, which was found in local clay deposits, in Loddiswell.

With the bounds of this parish enclosing some of the most stunning scenery in the South Hams, it is no wonder that Loddiswell preserves its independence. It still supports a number of small businesses, of which I will mention just a few.

YELLOW OCHRE

Both the interior and exterior of many cottages in the area were painted in yellow ochre, which was dug from fields named East Ochre, West Ochre and South Ochre. It came in two colours: yellow from the clay, and red where the ochre had been tinted by iron deposits. It was processed by John and Henry Luscombe, 'Refiners of Colours', around the 1830s. Still in the paint business, H. Luscombe and Son, at 19 Fore Street, Kingsbridge, remains a family business 160 years on.

Heron Valley Cider This fine cider is made nearby and can be bought in the village shop along with Steve Bradley's exceptional apple and refreshing grapefruit and apple juice (great with gin!).

Ham Farm Pete Hahn designs sumptuous hats, bags and coats: sculptural forms in felts and velvets saturated with royal colours. Carl Hahn makes unique, complex pieces of furniture. **Ring for an appointment ☎ 01548 550417.**

Hazelwood House

MGM Nurseries This family-run nursery grows a range of shrubs, herbaceous plants, alpines, trees, as well as bedding plants. They also stock a heady selection of David Austin roses. Liz and Malcolm Montague's smallholding, with ducks, chickens, goats and all sorts of birds, will be sure to divert non-gardeners, while those with 'the bug' get down to the serious business of plant buying. **MGM Nurseries, Woolston Lodge, Loddiswell ☎ 01548 550754.**

A Walk from Loddiswell

There are two possible places to begin this walk. The first (and longer) walk starts at Loddiswell Church, taking the old road which runs between Loddiswell and the river via Avon Mill—the second starting point for this glorious riverside woodland walk, which in spring is simply drenched with bluebells.

1. Loddiswell Church From the church, a lane runs down the back of the village. Traffic is scarce and the descent quite steep. The lane emerges at the Mill, the site of **Avon Mill Nursery**. It is possible to park a car here for a shorter woodland walk. This nursery has a wide selection of plants which are very well cared for. There is also the small but immensely popular **Tea Shop**, which also serves fine light lunches. The taking of cake here is an essential part of the outing—but should it be taken before or after the walk? **Avon Mill, Woodleigh Road ☎ 01548 550338.**

2. From **Avon Mill** turn left on to the road. It is little more than a five minute walk to Loddiswell Station, which is now a private house, The gateway into the woods is to the right of the station—marked 'Woodland Walk' on the OS map. This woodland was the first to be purchased by the Woodland Trust. Established by a local man called Charles Watkins, there are plans to plant a huge new woodland nearby in his memory. The route follows the old Primrose Line railway track, which once ran (briefly) between South Brent, Loddiswell and Kingsbridge. The going is fairly easy, and the fast-flowing Avon river alongside offers plenty of dipping and 'pooh sticks' opportunities. In Spring, the wood is carpeted with ramsons (wild garlic). Take a deep breath, and imagine you're in a French kitchen. Although few people collect it, it has been seen for sale at a famous deli in Covent Garden priced at £2.50 for a small bunch. Gather the strong-smelling leaves and just use as garlic, leeks or spring onion. Good in salads, in a cheese sandwich, or thrown in at the last minute in a creamy sauce to go with pasta.

The walk ends at Topsham Bridge, some two miles up the river. There's no option of a circular walk, so it's back the same way, but no less delightful in reverse.

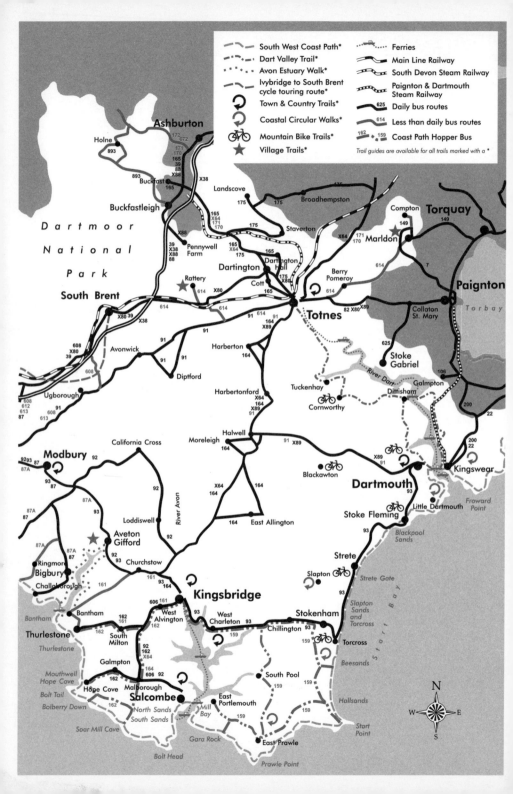

Transport

For a comprehensive guide to exploring the area by bus, ferry, train and on foot, pick up the Coast & Countryside Service's free *Out and About in the South Hams* leaflet—it's available from many local cafés, pubs and information centres. This section is based on *Out and About.*

Buses
The map shows the main bus routes in the area. For days out it's best to concentrate on the routes which offer more than one journey per day although you can with planning use less frequent services to advantage too. With improved and more frequent services this year it's even easier to use the bus.

When, where and how?
Most of the services in the area are operated by First Western National, but you will also find some routes served by Tally Ho! (around the Salcombe–Kingsbridge Estuary), Stagecoach Devon (Kingswear to Torbay), the Stoke Bus (Stoke Gabriel to Paignton only) and several community buses. For full details contact the company concerned or easier still, phone Devon County Council's 'Devonbus' enquiry line, open 8.30am–5.00pm Monday to Friday ☎ 01392 382800.

Cheaper Ways to Travel
There are lots of ways to cut the cost of travelling by bus.

• Day returns usually offer savings and can be bought on the bus.
• First Western National offer a day 'Explorer' ticket. Three or seven day 'Key West' tickets offer unlimited travel on both Stagecoach and First Western National Services throughout South Devon and Cornwall.
• The Dartmoor Sunday Rover ticket allows unlimited travel on all Dartmoor bus services on Sundays or bank holidays.
• If you are a senior citizen, a student aged 16–18 or a person with disabilities and you live in Devon, you should be eligible for a 'Countywide' bus pass which entitles you to half price fares throughout Devon. Phone the Countywide Enquiry Line ☎ 01392 383688 (calls charged at local rate) for full details.

Community Buses
Several community-run buses provide services from the more outlying villages into towns. If you live in the following villages, phone for details:

• The Coleridge bus links many villages on the east side of the Salcombe–Kingsbridge Estuary including Chillington, East Prawle, South Pool, Torcross, etc. Contact Barbara Jones ☎ 01548 852157.
• The Harbourne Shuttle links Ashprington, Cornworthy, Harbertonford, Halwell and Moreleigh to Totnes. Contact Alan Parsons ☎ 01803 712485.
• The West Dart Bus links Dittisham and Blackawton to Dartmouth, Totnes, Kingsbridge and Newton Abbot. ☎ 01803 712424.

Catch the Coast Path Hopper
In summer you can catch a bus to some of the most remote and spectacular stretches of the coast path. The special Coast Path Hopper (services 159 and 162) from Kingsbridge serves around 20 miles of coast path between Hope Cove and Torcross.

Full details, times and routes of the Hopper Bus (which runs from mid-May to September) will be available in the 'Out and About on the South Devon Coast' leaflet. This also gives details of other bus services which you can use to reach beaches and the coast path.

Bus Company Contact Numbers
First Western National ☎ 01752 222666 (open 7 days a week).
Tally Ho! ☎ 01548 853081.
Stagecoach Devon ☎ 01803 613226.
Stoke Bus ☎ 01803 554927.
Devon Bus ☎ 01392 382800.

Taxis
If you can't get a bus, consider taking a taxi. When there's a group of you, it can be cheaper than using a bus. Tourist Information Centres have lists of local taxi firms.

Cycle Hire
Cycle hire companies change fast. We therefore advise readers to contact their local Tourist Information Centre for a list of cycle hire companies.

Park and ride

If you're visiting the busy towns of Dartmouth or Salcombe by car in the summer, use the park and ride car parks and save petrol, time and the frustration of trying to park in town.

Dartmouth Park and Ride Located on the A381 approach road, just above Townstal. From 8.00 am to 6.15 pm, buses run every 15 minutes into town. A £2.50 all-day ticket allows parking and use of the park and ride bus all day. The park and ride operates from the 1st April to the beginning of October.

Salcombe Park and Ride Provides a regular service from the park and ride car park on the A381 approach road into the town, where you can be dropped right outside the shops.

The service operates between July and September. Parking and a bus ride to and from the town costs £2.00 for the day.

Crossing the Water

With five estuaries in the South Hams, ferries are an important and enjoyable way to get from place to place.

If you're walking the South West Coast Path, they form an essential link across the estuaries. Because ferries are dependent on tides and weather, we advise that you check the times and availability of ferry services (apart from the Dartmouth to Kingswear passenger ferries which run every day all year round) before travelling—especially small 'walkers ferries' across the Avon and Yealm. Phone the ferry operator, local harbour office or Tourist Information Centre for details. The table on the following pages will give you times and contact numbers for ferries across all the South Hams estuaries.

FERRY TIMETABLES

Type of Ferry	Operating Period	Operating times	Routes	Contact
RIVER AVON				
River Avon passenger ferry	17th April to 9th September	Mon–Sat 10–11am & 3–4pm. No Sunday service.	Bantham slipway to Cockleridge Ham (Bigbury-on-Sea)	Neil Schroeter 01548 561196 Mon–Fri 9am–4.30pm
SALCOMBE–KINGSBRIDGE ESTUARY				
Salcombe–East Portlemouth passenger ferry	all year	daily between 8am–5.30	Salcombe Pier (ferry steps) to East Portlemouth jetty	Ray Shortman 01548 842061
RIVER DART (1)				
Kingsbridge–Salcombe Estuary cruiser/passenger ferry	May–September	scheduled timetable (times vary according to tides—details from Tourist Info Centres	Kingsbridge town quay or Kingsbridge boatyard quay to Salcombe pier	Peter Moule (Rivermaid) 01548 853525/ 853607
Salcombe–South Sands passenger ferry	Easter–October	daily: half hourly service between 9.45am and 5.15pm	Salcombe pier (ferry steps), Salcombe Whitestrand, to South Sands beach	Tim Tucker 01548 561035
Lower Dartmouth vehicle ferry	daily all year	continuous service 7am–10.45pm (8am–10.55pm Sundays)	Kingswear to Dartmouth South Embankment	South Hams District Council 01803 752342
Higher Dartmouth vehicle ferry	daily all year	continuous service 6.30am–10.45pm (8am–11.45pm Sundays)	Dartmouth North Embankment to Kingswear Britannia Halt	Kerry Southern Philip 01803 833351

FERRY TIMETABLES

Type of Ferry	Operating Period	Operating times	Routes	Contact
RIVER DART (2)				
Dartmouth Castle passenger ferry	Easter–end October	daily 10am–5pm on demand— every few minutes when busy	Dartmouth South embankment to Dartmouth Castle	Julian Distin 01803 835034
Dartmouth– Dittisham passenger ferry	Over Easter, then Whitsun to end September	daily service— approx hourly between 10am–4.30pm (phone for times)	Dittisham pontoon & Dartmouth North Embankment	Dart Pleasure Craft (Dave Ridalls) 0781 8001108
Dittisham– Greenway passenger ferry	all year	daily: 7.30am–9pm summer (7.30am–5pm winter) on demand— ring bell at Dittisham to summon ferry or phone to book in advance	Dittisham & Greenway Quay—phone for links to Duncannon and Ashprington during the summer	Greenway Ferry Service (Frank Kirk) 01803 844010
Totnes– Dartmouth passenger cruisers	April–October	scheduled timetables (times vary with tides)— information on quaysides and Tourist Info Centres	between Totnes Steamer Quay & Dartmouth South embankment	River Link 01803 834488
Kingswear– Dartmouth passenger ferry	all year	daily regular service 7am–11pm (9am–11pm Sundays)	Dartmouth (by Station Restaurant) to Kingswear (by railway station	River Link 01803 834488

Seasonal Calendar

Participate in local events! Seasonal celebrations and events are usually advertised in the local papers (see opposite).

Spring
Spring flower arrangements in churches at Eastertime
Jumble sales
Bluebell woods at Loddiswell
Magnolia Campbellii at Overbecks
Crocus circle under the turkey oak at Dartington Hall Gardens
Easter fairs
Spring plant sales
Art Week in Dartmouth
Craft fairs
Gardens open to the public

Summer
Horticultural shows
Regattas and firework displays
Village fetes
Carnivals
Agricultural shows
Playgoers Shakespeare Production in Dartington Hall gardens
Ways with Words Literary Festival at Dartington Hall
Dartington Summer School of Music

Autumn
Raft Race on the River Dart
Harvest festivals and Harvest suppers
Village bonfire night celebrations
Riverford Farm's Pumpkin Day
Jumble sales

Winter
Fatstock shows
Village pantomimes
Church concerts
Christmas fairs: Dittisham Craft Fair, St Nicholas Fair in Kingsbridge

Information

Local Papers

South Hams Newspapers publish the following local papers every Friday: *Kingsbridge and Salcombe Gazette, Totnes Times,* and *Dartmouth Chronicle.* South Hams Newspapers ☎ 01548 853101.

Amongst other things, the local papers list events to come, as well as providing an insight into local issues and news. Regular features include:

What's On Listed in the 'What's On' section is news of local events: ram roasts, rambles, boot sales, jazz nights, dog shows, horticultural shows, gardens open, flower festivals, film showings, regattas etc.

Tide Times Listed under the information section on page six along with the duty chemists and firing times at HMS Cambridge are the times of high water GMT at Salcombe. These are vital for planning which beach to visit at what time, as well as the odd boat trip.

Tourist Information Centres

Kingsbridge The Quay, Kingsbridge ☎ 01548 853195.
Dartmouth: The Engine House, Mayors Avenue ☎ 01803 834224.
Totnes: The Town Mill ☎ 01803 863168.
Salcombe: Council Hall, Market Street ☎ 01548 843927.

Events

Events of all kinds are run by various organisations the year round. It would be wise to find out what's going on in advance of a visit to the South Hams, as booking is advisable.

National Trust

Talks walks and performances are programmed at National Trust properties. Enquiries and information ☎ 01392 881691.

Coast and Countryside Events

Paddle down the Avon, pick your own wild food supper, paint from earth pigments, try a seashore safari, see a traditional wassail or listen to local stories. . . . Trudy Turrell and the team produce an increasingly irresistible programme of events for all seasons. Pick up a programme at local village shops and Tourist Information Centres, and book early. For details ☎ 01803 861140.

English Heritage
The English Heritage diary of special events runs between April and the end of October, featuring activities, events and entertainments at sites in Dartmouth and Totnes. These include the hardy group of Living History players, who set up camp at Dartmouth Castle and live and eat 17th century-style, with occasional frenzied firing of muskets as re-enactments of civil war battles rage around the castle walls. For information on these and other events contact Dartmouth Castle ☎ 01803 833588 or Totnes Castle ☎ 01803 684406.

Slapton Ley Field Studies Centre
Regular walks and nature safaris are run during the summer months in and around the exceptional nature reserve at Slapton. Ideal for families. ☎ 01548 580466.

The Ramblers Association (see Kingsbridge outings)
They hold regular walks in and around the South Hams. For details contact the General Secretary, Mr Basil Fox ☎ 01548 561419, or contact the local Tourist Information Centre for details.

Gardens Open to the Public
Each year the National Gardens Scheme publish a 'yellow book', which details dates and times of Devon gardens open to the public. Available in bookshops and TICs.

Auctions
Notice of forthcoming auction sales around one week before the sale. Regular auctions of furniture and effects are held at Dartmouth and Kingsbridge. Kingsbridge Auction Sales hold sales at the Market hall around the second Thursday of the month starting at 10.00 am. Viewing is on the Wednesday 9.00 am–4.00 pm. Enquiries ☎ 01548 85682.

In Dartmouth, regular auctions are held at The Old Sorting Office Hauley Road. Viewing is spread over three days with the auction on the Thursday—again around the middle of the month. Enquiries to Daphne Scorer ☎ 01803 835007.

Booklist

Along the Dart by Judy Chard, Bossiney Books, 1979.
The Birds and Natural History of the South Hams by Gordon Waterhouse, Orchard Books, 2000.
The Book of Loddiswell: a photographic history of the Parish, Halsgrove Press, 1999.
Dartmouth and its Neighbours by Ray Freeman, Phillimore, 1990.
Dartmouth—a Brief Historical Guide by Tom Jaine, Dartmouth & Kingswear Society, 1996.
Dittisham Village Guide, Dittisham Parish Council, revised 1996.
Devon Building by Peter Beacham, Devon Books, 1990.
The Elmhirsts of Dartington by Michael Young, Routledge & Kegan Paul, 1982, reprinted by Dartington Hall Trust, 1996.
A Fortunate Place: A History of Slapton by Robin Stanes, Field Studies Council, 1983.
The Good Town of Totnes by Percy Russell, Devonshire Association, 1963.
Hallsands: a Pictorial History by Sugden Designs, 1984.
History of Kingsbridge and Salcombe by Ann Born, Phillimore, 1986.
Kingsbridge, Devon by Ann Born & Kathy Tanner, 1986.
Kingsbridge and surroundings, Sarah Prideaux Fox, 1874.
Kingsbridge Estuary with rambles in the neighbourhood, Sarah Prideaux Fox, 1864, reprinted by Cookworthy Museum 1982.
Magic Tree: Devon Garden Plants—History and Conservation, Devon Books/NCCPG 1989.
Salcombe and Neighbourhood by James Fairweather, third edition, 1912.
Story of Thurlestone, Bantham & West Buckland by Kendal McDonald, 1993.
The Tragedy of Hallsands Village by John L Harvey.
Wildlife of the Dart Estuary by Tony Soper, Harbour Books, 1982.
Wildlife of the Kingsbridge & Salcombe Estuary by Gordon Waterhouse Orchard Books, 1999.

Also recommended: Coast & Countryside Town and Village Trails for Totnes, Kingsbridge, Dartmouth and Aveton Gifford; and Coast & Countryside Walks leaflets. All available from Tourist Information Centres (see above).

Index

142

OFF THE MAP

Hot Pursuit Bikes,
Totnes 102
hotels 17, 25, 27-8, 34-5,
42-3, 79
Hunters Lodge Inn,
Cornworthy 91

information 137-8
insects 11, 118, 122, 125
Island Cruising Club,
Salcombe 36, 37, 46

Jarvis, Richard 44
Jon Alsop Sailmaker 36
Jordan, Richard 43

Ken's Kitchen,
Kingsbridge 58
Kingfisher Fish & Chips
103
Kingsbridge 50-9
Kingsbridge Estuary 45-
64, 134
Kingswear 85-6
Kingswear Castle 86
Kitchen Garden,
Salcombe 37
kite flying 117, 124

Lack, David 112
Ladies Cove, Dartmouth
85
Leach, Bernard 108
leisure centres 34, 56,
103
Lescaze, William 110
Lidstones, Kingsbridge
51
lime kilns 60, 62, 82,
83, 109
local events 20, 48-9,
52-3, 73-5, 77, 113, 114-
15, 128, 136-8
Loddiswell 126, 127-9
Loft Restaurant, Sorley
64-5

Loft Studio, Salcombe
36
Longmarsh 106-7
Lower North Mill 12, 14
Luccombe, William 110,
114
Luscombe, A.W., Totnes
104
Luscombe, H.,
Kingsbridge 127

Maltsters Arms,
Tuckenhay 95
Mange Tout,
Kingsbridge 58
Marine Hotel, Salcombe
32, 34-5
marine life 15, 45, 47
markets 53, 55-6
Marshall Arts, Totnes
100
Masefield, John 12, 13
Mattiscombe Beach 28
McCrum, Bridget 90
Meals on Keels,
Dartmouth 73
Mercer, Ian 112
MGM Nurseries,
Loddiswell 128
Milburns, Kingsbridge
54
Millbrook, South Pool
50
Molyneux, Joyce 78
Montagu, George 61
Murdoch, Tony 40-1
museums 33, 40, 57,
106

Natural Health Centre,
Totnes 103
naturism 14
Nicholson's Wholefood
& Health Shop 59
Nicola's, Kingsbridge 54
Nonsuch, Kingsbridge
54

North Sands 34
Number Seven, Totnes
100
nurseries 23, 38, 90-1,
127-8

Ocean Spirit, Salcombe
36
Oil Seller, Salcombe 36
Old Mill Creek 80-2
Orestone 12, 14
Overbeck, Otto 39-40
Overbecks 39-41
Oyster House,
Bigbury-on-Sea 121-2
Oyster Shack, Bigbury
121

papermaking 82-3, 94
Paperworks, Totnes 101
parks 34, 57
Pedlar's Pack, Totnes
102
Petroc, Saint 84
Pig Finca, Kingsbridge
55
plants 14, 15-16, 18, 22,
48, 118, 121, 125, 128-
9
Portlemouth Pastries,
Kingsbridge 58
pottery 82-3, 108, 109
Prawle Point 38
priories 91-2
Prismatic, Totnes 100
pubs 21, 22, 25, 48, 58,
89-90, 91, 95, 119

Quick, Margaret and
Peter 63

raft races 115
recipes 85, 87, 129
Recycle, Totnes 102
Red Arrows 74, 75
Red Lion Inn, Dittisham
89